RECONSTRUCTING
CHRISTIANITY

For Sue
(Proverbs 5:18-19)

RECONSTRUCTING CHRISTIANITY

✦

Notes from the New Reformation

Rich Mayfield

iUniverse, Inc.

New York Lincoln Shanghai

RECONSTRUCTING CHRISTIANITY
Notes from the New Reformation

iUniverse books may be ordered through booksellers or by contacting:

iUniverse
2021 Pine Lake Road, Suite 100
Lincoln, NE 68512
www.iuniverse.com
1-800-Authors (1-800-288-4677)

ISBN-13: 978-0-595-37298-0 (pbk)
ISBN-13: 978-0-595-81696-5 (ebk)
ISBN-10: 0-595-37298-8 (pbk)
ISBN-10: 0-595-81696-7 (ebk)

Printed in the United States of America

INTRODUCTION

Anyone with even a touch of interest in religious anthropology knows that humanity's history is filled with a yearning to bond with the eternal. All kinds of methods and means have been created to satisfy that yearning. They are called religions. My religion, Christianity, developed the understanding that our bond with God could only be accomplished by the sacrificial death of Jesus. This understanding shaped our theology for centuries. Most of our old hymns and many of our teachings are profoundly shaped by this conception. But that is changing. For some of us it is ancient history. We have discovered that Christianity is not bound to a primeval world-view or a religion shaped by ancient cultural practices. This is a new day. This is a new Christianity. It continues to express a yearning for God yet this expression is found not in bizarre pre-modern beliefs but in contemporary symbols and convictions. The cross is not an instrument for appeasing an angry God but a symbol of the unconditional love that is the hallmark of God. The altar which once served as a base for sacrifice has now turned into a table to feed all who come. The font, which once depicted the need to wash off our humanity, now welcomes us with its symbol of the fundamental element of human life.

What follows are simply some notes I have made along the way to this new Christianity. As in my first book, "Confessions of a Christian Agnostic", I have arranged them to be read a day at a time. My intention is that they serve as thought-provokers and discussion-starters. My hope is that they will serve to open up a whole new way of understanding this faith of ours. I welcome your comments and I invite you into conversation. I am convinced that there is indeed a New Reformation occurring in Christianity and I am eager to share it with you.

Rich Mayfield

JANUARY 1

It is interesting to note that the word Christian is found in the Christian scriptures only three times. The word "disciple" however is found 269 times. Disciple and discipline, of course, come from the same source. To be a disciple is to be someone willing to accept the discipline of a particular way of life. It is a daunting word, I know, but it is also a realistic one. To be a disciple is to accept the responsibility for the care of your soul. No one can do it for us. The frantic nature of our lives isn't about to change without a change going on inside each of us.

JANUARY 2

Often I am accused of picking and choosing those parts of the Bible that please me and discarding those parts that don't. "Guilty as charged"...and I make no apology for it. I make no apology because that is what Judaism, Christianity and Islam have been doing since the very beginnings. Ancient editors picked and chose what to include in the Torah. Storytellers shortly after Jesus' death were deciding what stories were worth retelling and which ones weren't. Surely Jesus told many more stories than the few recorded in the gospels. Surely Jesus filled his days with far more activities than the couple hundred reported in the Bible. We're always picking and choosing! We should make no apology for that. Indeed, I believe, it is precisely what keeps our faith alive and vital. Jesus was constantly putting his disciples into new contexts and offering new solutions. He continues to do that with all those who dare to accept his invitation to: "Follow me."

JANUARY 3

"I want to die young…as late in life as possible."

My friend Dr. Paul Hamilton said that to me many years ago.

It is a wonderful philosophy of life and, I dare say, it is a very Christian one. To be young is to be inquisitive, hopeful, confident, bold. These are the marks, I am convinced, of discipleship. These are also the qualities that take each day and fill it full of adventure. When we stop growing we start dying. So much of Christianity is dying these days because we have forgotten the very life and teachings of Jesus. We have tried to take what is dynamic and make it doctrinaire. We have attempted to take what is vibrant and lively and turn it into something rigid and regimented. One of the exciting elements of this journey of faith for me is the unqualified invitation from Jesus to enter fully into the gifts of this life filled with the confidence that nothing I can do, say or believe will separate me from his wondrous love. This is the gospel. This is the good news.

JANUARY 4

The New Reformation is, I believe, as dramatic and profound as the one Luther led 500 years ago. And just as Dr. Martin had no real idea where it would all lead, most of the instigators of this reformation are equally in the dark. What they are clear about, however, is just how important this movement is to the future of Christianity.

There are many, of course, who would say that Christianity is fine just the way it is. They might point to churches that are filled to overflowing each Sunday with literally thousands of people, churches that have multi-million dollar budgets and staffs that can number into the hundreds. I would only comment that at the time Martin Luther began questioning the health and well-being of his church, there were congregations equally well endowed. Indeed, Luther may have wondered, as many of us have wondered, how the stark and sacrificial message of Jesus could so easily appeal to the masses. Might it be that this message has been subsumed into a religion that has less to do with the teachings of Jesus and far more to do with the traditional teachings about Jesus? Many of us would say that is exactly what has happened and we are bent on reclaiming, as best we can, the authentic teachings of Jesus unhindered by the inevitable biases laid upon them over the past two thousand years.

JANUARY 5

Do I believe that Jesus is the Son of God? I do indeed but this is a Son who is understood best by those who have been more the victims than the victorious. This is a Son who is recognized most fully by those who have been rejected most cruelly. This is a Son who stands with the poor, the weak, the rejected. This is a Son whose image is reflected in the eyes of a child dying of hunger or a mother dying of AIDS. This is a Son whose face is the same as the centurion who killed him, or the Iraqi who is about to die. This is Jesus the Son of God. May we have the courage to follow where he leads.

JANUARY 6

I have never gone in for astrology. I know that there are millions of good honest people who carefully read their horoscope each day but I have never had even the slightest of interest. I suspect it has not a little to do with my fervent belief in the freedom of the will. Any hint that my life is on some pre-determined course is repugnant to me and so I ignore what many people take seriously. I mention all of this because of the strange story in the Gospel of Matthew of some astrologers who, over the course of tradition and time, have come to be known as the Three Wise Men. Odd it is that these practitioners of the occult have for two thousand years been lifted up as being unusually wise and gifted men even though they come from what would clearly be called a pagan perspective on life.

They are seekers after truth is who these wise men are. The Bible respects such searching and even though these three come looking for the truth from another way, they are elevated by their honest inquiry. This is a key and crucial point that I don't want any of us to miss. There is in the New Testament an inherent honor for those who search for the truth, no matter how they go about their searching. Even Paul, who normally doesn't suffer pagans gladly, is reported to have said to the Athenians, "I perceive that you are very religious." (Acts 17) Such a compliment to those who worship pagan gods! But the very fact that they are searching is worthy of Paul's and our respect. So, too, for these strange astrologers from the East. So, too, I am convinced, for all those who search for truth in ways different than our own.

JANUARY 7

How we have taken a message that began as inclusive, open, honest and loving and turned it into a message of legalism, exclusion and fear is one of the great mysteries of Christianity. Actually it isn't that mysterious. Its human. It's our innate human tendency to want to horde what we have and not share it with others. It's the sad reality that most of us operate out of a mindset of scarcity rather than abundance. It is as if we believe that there is only so much of God to go around so we'd better keep most of God to ourselves. God is reserved only for those who think like us, look like us, act like us and, most importantly, believe exactly like us.

Thank goodness Jesus shows us what a lot of hokum that is. That is why I am convinced that Jesus discovered a truth that was greater than John the Baptist's. It went from a religion for the few to a God for all. It reached out beyond the boundaries of a particular religious practice and proclaimed that everyone was welcome. It isn't that John the Baptist was wrong so much as that Jesus was so much more right.

JANUARY 8

It is my assumption that most if not all of Jesus' teachings were done not in the manner of the college lecturer but the neighborhood rabbi. Over and over again, we can find evidence that Jesus responded to the questions and inquiries of his followers not with words of advice as much as stories. What does it mean to love your neighbor? Jesus tells the story of the Good Samaritan. What does it mean to love unconditionally? Jesus tells the story of the Prodigal Son. Such responses were in keeping with the traditions of Judaism, indeed with most great religious teachers.

And how frustrating that must have been! For I suspect the folks of Jesus' day weren't much different than us. They liked nice neat answers. A simple yes or no would suffice. Instead they and we are stuck with the nuance and subtleties of story.

JANUARY 9

Most folk know that the accounts of Jesus' resurrection in the Bible are markedly different. Mark's account, the oldest, has only an empty tomb. Matthew has Jesus making his appearance in Galilee a full week's journey away from Jerusalem. Luke has the risen Christ asking his disciples for something to eat...a bodily need if ever there was one. Different accounts. Different impressions by different artists. Is one right and the others wrong? Of course not. This is not science. This is spirituality. These are not rules for religion but invitations to a relationship, a relationship with a God whose power of love is so great that nothing can stop it, not even death.

JANUARY 10

For over seven years, I have had a website on the Internet entitled: "Confessions of a Christian Agnostic" and at least once a week someone will e-mail me with the same question/accusation: "How can you be both a Christian and an agnostic?" And I always reply: "How can you not?"

A guidepost for Progressive Christianity is the realization that there is more grace in the search for truth than in dogmatic certainty. When someone tells you they've got it all figured out...even if they're all dressed up in the finest of churchy robes....run in the other direction. Those are the folk out to put a muzzle on the truth. Think about the terrible scandals in recent church history. How did they come to be? Certainly in part because people were afraid to raise their hand and ask a question. Certainly in part because folk were thinking you can't be a Christian and also be an agnostic.

JANUARY 11

What's the big deal anyway? We know they're only words.

But, you see, in our world words are very important. They are one of the means for conveying truth, establishing relationships, working for good. We must be exceedingly careful as to how they are used. One of the biggest lies ever perpetrated is "Sticks and stones will break my bones but words will never hurt me." The way we use words in the church is hurting millions of people and preventing them from hearing the good news of God's immeasurable love in a language that they can understand.

JANUARY 12

Our picture of Jesus and the disciples has a definite chauvinistic tint to it. All the disciples are men, we are told, although even the Bible can't seem to agree on exactly who was a part of the actual twelve. But if we read a little closer we may find some intriguing hints that things weren't exactly as we might have thought.

For instance, in I Corinthians, Chapter 9, Paul indicates that the disciples, including Peter and the brothers of Jesus, all brought their wives along with them. And over and over again in the accounts we have, women are present, indeed women seem to play an important role…even providing for the disciples out of their own means.

How intriguing that women seem to have played a much larger role in the formative stages of Christianity than we have been led to believe. Further, how intriguing that women were so quickly denigrated as the church became more and more institutionalized until, before we knew it, all the clergy have to be men…and celibate to boot!

Women have moved from being right at Jesus' side to pushed out the back door.

JANUARY 13

One of the very saddest things I ever hear, and I will tell you I hear it far too often is, "Its just the way I am." I hear it from a husband who is willing to let his marriage fall apart rather than open up. I hear it from a lonely lady who would rather bear a grudge than forgive. I even hear it from the Christian who is so set in his ways he'd miss out on the Resurrected Christ if he were right in the room with him. Life, it seems to me, is change or it just isn't life at all but some kind of terrible hell of sameness and death. To imagine an unchanging life in an unchanging world is to imagine the most horrific of scenarios.

And yet this is precisely what far too many of us want with our religion. We want it to be the same as it was last week, last year, last century. "Give me that old-time religion. It's good enough for me." But it shouldn't be. Because just as you have grown and matured, just as you, like it or not, have changed, so has the world in which your faith lives. If your faith continues to be mired down in 18th century science or 15th century language or 1st century mores, it is terribly susceptible to becoming an irrelevant faith that belongs in a museum and not out here in the real world.

JANUARY 14

Somewhere along the line Christianity confused itself by taking up the claim that this religion was all about personal salvation. I submit it is just the opposite. It is about the salvation of the world, of all people, all nations, all cultures. It is about community. It is about compassion. It is about identifying with those different than us. To take what Jesus taught and turn it into something so sinister is the very definition of blasphemy in my mind.

I am passionate about this because I believe this kind of religious thinking is the most dangerous force at work in the world today. It matters little if it comes from Christians, Jews or Muslims. It matters not if the scripture is Hebrew, Christian or the Qur'an. It doesn't matter if it comes through best-selling books or box-office hit movies. It is a perversion of the teachings of Jesus and it needs to be opposed. Not by force but by our faith in a loving God. Not by violence but by our conviction in the power of non-violence. Not by ridicule but reason. But oppose it we must for the sake of the world that God so loved.

January 15

In the middle of the last century, a Catholic theologian by the name of Karl Rahner devised a term that, although I am not completely comfortable with it, I find helpful in discerning the essence of the teachings of Jesus. "Anonymous Christians" is how Rahner described those people not officially associated with the Christian Church but acting in a manner that would identify them as disciples, knowingly or not, of Jesus. In other words, the atheists in Holland who hid Jewish boys and girls from the Nazis were "anonymous Christians". The young man or woman who eschews religion but serves in the Peace Corps working against the ravages of AIDS is an "anonymous Christian". Indeed, the Iraqi doctor who binds the wounds of enemy soldiers just as that Good Samaritan did for the Jew on the side of the road is an "anonymous Christian." Can such a designation help us understand the radical nature of Jesus' ministry? It was a ministry designed not to prove who is right or who is wrong but to call us all to lives of compassion and peace.

JANUARY 16

This is a little prayer technique I learned from another of my mentors, Matthew Fox. He has you all standing and stretching up to the sky and then down to the earth. Up and down. And then breathe in when you go up and breathe out when you go down. Breathe in the spirit of hope. Breathe out feelings of despair. Breathe in love for creation. Breathe out the need to dominate or subdue. Breathe in compassion for others. Breathe out fear of the unknown. Breathe in acceptance of differences. Breathe out the need to be right. Breathe in a welcome to strangers. Breathe out all boundaries and borders. Breathe in the presence of Jesus. Breathe out our prejudices and preconceptions. Breathe in the energy of the earth and all of creation. Breathe out your hurts and resentments. Breathe in. Breathe out. Amen.

JANUARY 17

Ecclesia reformata: the reforming church, the re-forming church.

This is, I believe to the depths of my being, what it means to be a disciple, what it means to follow Jesus, what it means to be a Christian. When the church stops reforming it stops being the church. It may be a beautiful museum or an inspiring mausoleum but it is not the church. And there are a lot of museums and mausoleums passing themselves off as something they're not these days.

JANUARY 18

You may be surprised to learn that there are something like 50 other gospels that never made it into the Bible. By about 185 CE the list had been whittled down to the four we know but there were some congregations who continued to use some of these alternative gospels.

Recently the Gospel of Thomas has received a great deal of attention by biblical scholars for what it reveals to us of these Christians who were outside the mainstream. It wasn't until 367 CE that the New Testament was canonized, that is, officially authorized by a gathering of Christian leaders. The books are sacred because the church made them so.

The Bible, like all sacred texts, didn't come from the sky down but from the ground up. It is the recollections, understandings, biases, of a particular people in a particular time.

JANUARY 19

So much of Christianity, it seems to me, is dependent on a Christ who is anything but a failure, anything but an outcast, anything but a loser who ends up like a common crook hanging from a cross. Not long ago someone came to me to explain why they no longer were going to come to church. "I want a happy-go-lucky Christianity," he said to me. A happy-go-lucky Christianity? That must mean Christianity without the cross, Christianity without the crucifixion, a Christianity where Jesus skips Calvary and lives happily ever after with his band of merry men.

Too much of Christianity has been turned into a kind of self-help guide to personal success. The bookshelves are filled with volumes that promise all kinds of pleasures for anyone willing to accept a Christianity that doesn't accept failure. But the Jesus of scripture does fail. Not in the end perhaps but we cannot brush aside the fact that living a life of love does not always result in earthly rewards. Jesus chose to bring the outsiders in and with them came a whole lot of trouble. He broke the rules. He went outside the lines. He thought for himself. He chose to be vulnerable. He was willing to err on the side of grace. And so he was killed. Following the God of love does not guarantee a happy-go-lucky lifestyle.

JANUARY 20

I remember a story Mother Teresa told of discovering that there was a Hindu family near her who had no food. So gathering what she could, Mother Teresa took her bucket of beans and rice and visited the family. Having said thanks, the Hindu mother then divided the food and took half of it to a hungry Muslim family nearby.

JANUARY 21

I find it most disturbing to have Jesus saying: "All who came before me are thieves and bandits." (John 10:8)

I don't know about you, but from my understanding of the life and teachings of Jesus, this just doesn't fit.

Does this mean that John the Baptist is a thief? Does this mean Moses is a bandit? I don't believe for a moment that such sentiment ever crossed the lips of Jesus.

What I do believe is that the author of John is trying, perhaps too desperately, to advocate the supremacy of Jesus. It is his intention not just to honor Jesus' life and teaching but to convince us that Jesus is divine. His efforts, well intended as they may be, are precisely that, well-intended efforts. We are not obligated to accept them as fact.

Can we say that? I hope so because it is only then that we can begin to truly integrate the great gift of Jesus into our lives. When Christianity demands that we accept what we know isn't true, it is no longer Christianity, it is no longer a gift of Jesus.

A Christianity that forces us to be false to what we believe in our hearts has no business calling itself holy.

January 22

The front page this week was filled with one horror story after another of the conflict between Israel and Palestine. Here in the very place where that first Easter was experienced, hardly a day goes by without another horrifying report of more innocent people killed. I suspect that many of you, like me, have wondered if this is simply an unsolvable problem. As long as people are bent on revenge, committed to an eye for an eye, people will continue to die, both the innocent and the guilty. As long as people cling to ways that have always been, patterns of behavior that haven't changed for centuries, then continued killing is inevitable. The daily slaughter will go on and on and on. What needs to die, you see, is not the enemy. What needs to die are the patterns of behavior that have shaped these cultures for thousands of years. What needs to die is the clinging to old ways of doing things, old ways of explaining things, old ways that result in nothing new but dead bodies. It doesn't take a genius to recognize that what is needed here is resurrection. What is needed here is a new way of thinking, a new way of living, a new way of understanding. What is needed here is a new creation and it can only come when the old ways are allowed to die and be buried.

JANUARY 23

The Bible was written, from beginning to end, by men…inspired, we are always quick to add, by God.

Only we should also remember that it is a God defined too often and too narrowly by men and for men.

Although it is changing, the Church has been controlled by men for all of its life. Isn't it interesting then that the one important woman in all of Christian scriptures is turned into something other than a real woman? It is as if the men in control found the very thought that God would lower HIMSELF in such a crude way so repugnant they immediately began a campaign of denial. The campaign has continued nearly unabated for two thousand years.

It is time for it to end. The miracle of Christ is not found in Bethlehem but on Calvary. Jesus does not reveal God in magical beginnings but in painfully real endings. "This is the way to the kingdom of heaven." Jesus says, and then guides us into a life of ordinary human interactions. A life of loving others, forgiving others, feeding, liberating, empowering others…all in the name of the God of the ordinary.

JANUARY 24

In the Metropolitan Museum of Art there is a painting, I forget the artist, that depicts the ascension. It shows the disciples all looking up. At the top of the frame are two feet on their way skyward. It is hard not to view this work without smiling. The artistic literalism can't help but evoke humorous captions and semi-snide commentary on the superstitions of the faith. The problem for Christians, of course, is not to throw the baby out with the bath water. The problem is to reclaim the message even if we must discard the messenger. What is so marvelous about that painting is the look on the disciples' faces. They seem to be saying, "What do we do now?" "Where do we go from here?" Those are the pivotal, the crucial, questions of Christianity today.

JANUARY 25

I believe in ritual. This is something that grows stronger as the years go by. Of all my roles as preacher, teacher, pastor and more, it is being a priest that brings the greatest meaning for me. To assist others in expressing awe, wonder, mystery and more is an enormous privilege that I cherish and am certain will be difficult to give up. I grieve for our world and its failure to see the beauty of ritual well thought and carefully performed. As someone who has presided over countless weddings, baptisms, funerals and more I can attest to the palpable power that is unleashed in ritual. The reason so many of us pooh-pooh it is precisely that power. We don't know what to do with our tears, our feelings that come flooding out when we confront the profundity of life, the mystery of the universe. Ritual gives us an avenue, a way of entering deeply into the richness of creation, the depth of our lives. At its best, Christianity, like all religions, provides a place for humanity and God to meet.

JANUARY 26

I take enormous pleasure in opening a new jar of peanut butter. I love twisting that lid for the first time and feeling that little tug of resistance that precedes the turn. It is almost as if the jar wants to ask if I really am going to appreciate all the good that's sitting inside. Then there is that foil seal that separates me from the peanut blended concoction. I cut it carefully around the edge until my finger and thumb can get a good hold and then, ever so slowly, I peel it back to reveal the silky brown smoothness of untouched peanut butter beauty. No knife with little remnants of strawberry jam has yet to pierce that pristine and perfect peanut butter landscape. I stand at the counter and breathe in my pleasure. Is there a prayer for this occasion in the Lutheran Book of Worship? There should be. It is such a good thing.

JANUARY 27

"Just As I Am".

Most everyone who has ever set foot in a church knows this old chestnut. It's the one Billy Graham has played each time he calls folk down to the front of the stage to be born again. A real old favorite. Only it really isn't very old in the overall scheme of things. This one was written in the mid-19th century, a bastion of similar hymnody that proclaims a very particular understanding of the work of Jesus.

"Just as I am without one plea, but that thy blood was shed for me, and that thou bidd'st me come to thee, O lamb of God I come, I come. Just as I am and waiting not to rid my soul of one dark blot, to thee whose blood can cleanse each spot, O Lamb of God, I come, I come."

Most familiar and it is most indicative of a strain of Christianity that took hold particularly among American Protestants in the 19th and 20th centuries. It depicts the central theme of sin and redemption that so many understand as the sum and total of Christianity. And yet as we work our way back, closer to the very time of Jesus, we discover other understandings, other descriptions of what it means to be a Christian.

JANUARY 28

The sign was big, so big, in fact, that you could see it from every corner of the intersection. I was stuck behind two dozen cars waiting for the light to turn green and couldn't help pondering the sign and its proclamation. It was a sign for a church and it announced not only the name of the church and its worship times along with a list of its pastors but at the bottom in bold and cursive script it said, "Everyone Welcome!"

Sitting there slowly inching my way toward the light, I thought about that sign, particularly its concluding announcement. Although some might find such an invitation to be most congenial and, indeed, hospitable, I couldn't help but speculate on the odd necessity of a church having to declare such a thing to begin with. "Everyone welcome!" surely should be a statement of redundancy when referring to a church. Of course, it only took me a nanosecond or two to realize, with sadness, how very untrue that is. The truth be told, the church can be one of the most unwelcoming institutions in America today.

JANUARY 29

I have never been particularly drawn to a religion that glosses over the gory or glibly excuses the tragic. I suppose that is why I am grateful that so many of the psalms don't either. Yes, there are psalms that could be categorized as "happy-clappy" but they comprise less than a third of the collection. Most of the others recognize a complexity to life that shallow spirituality just cannot address. The popularity of Psalm 23 surely comes not just in its beautiful artistic images but also in its honest confrontation with reality. "The shadow of death" looms over us. Each and every one of us must walk through it. Trusting that God walks with us is the very essence of what Jesus meant by peace. It is not a peace of blissed out passivity but a peace that openly acknowledges the struggles that all of us endure. We are not alone, the psalmist sings. That is grace. That is the message of Christ.

JANUARY 30

Once Thomas Merton prayed, "My Lord God, I have no idea where I am going, I do not see the road ahead of me, I cannot know for certain where it will end. Nor do I really know myself and the fact that I think I am following your will does not mean that I am actually doing so. But I believe that the desire to please you does in fact please you." Do you find that as liberating, as exhilarating as I do? There is no wrong way to God. Nor is there a "right" way. There is only God. There is only love. If your love is growing, if your awareness of God's love for you is growing, you are growing into God. You are entering into the kingdom.

JANUARY 31

One of the great sorrows in my work is watching imagination die. I speak with a couple and they can no longer imagine a meaningful marriage. I talk with a friend and he can no longer imagine a job that is satisfying.

It is the death of hope and it is the ultimate tragedy.

When we in the church can no longer imagine a God who welcomes change and growth, who no longer invites an imaginative spirit, who no longer calls us to follow into the future but only believe in the past, the church is dying and God is already dead.

FEBRUARY 1

I have long advocated that the only understanding of heaven that I can fathom is a heaven where everyone is there…Christian, Jew, Muslim, Buddhist, Agnostic, Atheist, everyone. It is the only image that is in keeping with the teachings of Jesus. Two nice women came to see me some years ago, Bibles in hand, to convince me of the error of my ways. We talked for awhile and, I suppose, they finally decided I was hopeless. As they left one of these sweeties turned to me and said, "How sad it will be when we get to heaven and you won't be there." I replied, "It won't be heaven unless I am there!" God's love is for everyone or it isn't for anyone. As far as I can tell, Jesus never played favorites. Neither should we.

FEBRUARY 2

In her epic work, "The History of God", Karen Armstrong portrays the evolutionary nature of our faith, how it emerged in a world of many gods and slowly, ever so slowly, consolidated these various images into one image, one god. Jesus offered his own perception. Paul offered his as well. The gospel writers brought theirs and then the early church fathers, then Augustine, then Luther, then Dr. King, then Bishop Spong…and on and on to this very day, new images, new insights, new ways of discerning what we have come to call holy, what we have come to call God. This is precisely why we call this a journey, a journey of discovery, a journey into God.

FEBRUARY 3

"It was the best of times, it was the worst of times."

Dickens, of course, was describing the French Revolution, a time filled with ambiguity. Liberty and freedom walked hand in hand with violence and deep despair. Certainly this line could be used for any period in history but I do think it is particularly appropriate to today's world. We stand in the midst of incredible prosperity and wealth here in America and at the same time we are surrounded by hunger and poverty. Daily we are witness to newspaper accounts of death and destruction. Daily we read of the horrors inflicted upon innocent children by the ravages of hunger, poverty, AIDS, despots. Daily we confront such horrors from the comfort of our homes. It is the best of times, it is the worst of times.

FEBRUARY 4

"Gee, I didn't know I could believe that!"

It has been offered in a myriad of different ways that include surprise, joy, excitement, and utter shock. Most often it is followed by a conversation that will include a most important reminder and one that I underscore today. It is this: All talk of God is and always will be in metaphor. That is, to describe the God who is by definition greater than we can ever know, we must employ the similes and metaphors of our own language and time to say what God is like rather than what God actually is. So, for instance, when we employ the image of father in our prayers, we are not actually describing a physical being with the characteristics of a male member of the human species but rather an image, a metaphor for what we imagine God to be like, a loving father. These metaphors are found throughout our scripture and tradition. God is a wind or a mighty fortress or a good shepherd. These images don't define God but only describe our feelings about God. Most of these metaphors were developed in a different time and place, a different culture, employing a very different language. Some of the metaphors continue to resonate for many of us and some do not. What is important to remember is that they are metaphors not scientific descriptions. The traditional manner in which Christians describe this God using metaphor is Father, Son and Holy Spirit. For nearly two thousand years this has served many quite well and allowed pilgrims on the journey to achieve a kind of understanding of the work of God. But it is not a final or ultimate definition of God. It is only a description employing our own limited resources. In recent years, I have heard faithful Christians use other metaphors…"creator, redeemer, sustainer" for instance or "the voice, the word, the listener". These and many others are legitimate uses of metaphor as they speak to an evolving, ever-changing faith.

FEBRUARY 5

"What have you to do with us?" asks the demon of Jesus. It is my question as well. Raising our families, earning our livings, making our decisions...what has Jesus to do with any of this? It is much easier, of course, to keep Jesus at a distance, relegated to a quick hour on a Sunday morning or an even quicker prayer right before we fall asleep. What has Jesus to do with us anyway? It certainly makes life confusing with his meddling in everything. Much better to keep him confined inside those gold edged pages of the dusty leather book.

FEBRUARY 6

Look at the first writings in the New Testament. They are by Paul, written at least two decades before any of the gospels and representing much of what was going on in the early church. No mention of the life of Jesus. None. No Good Samaritan story. No Prodigal Son story. No Beatitudes or blessings of children. None of that. There is only the death and resurrection. Look at the creeds that were written a few hundred years later. What do they say about the life and teachings of Jesus? Not much. "Born of the Virgin Mary. He suffered under Pontius Pilate, was crucified, died and was buried." What happened to those thirty years in between? That's what fascinates me and many other folk who dare to call themselves Christians. Tell us about his teachings! Tell us about his parables, his promises, his pictures of the kingdom! This is what captured his disciples and changed their lives. Surely it can do the same for us as well.

FEBRUARY 7

The New Reformation is about returning to the faith of Jesus. It is about recapturing the image of God that Jesus certainly had and sharing it with a church that has too often missed it. It's about recognizing how easy it is to be a religion centered on John the Baptist's condemnation rather than Jesus' invitation.

I love the line in Luke's gospel where Jesus surely must have smiled when he said, "Look you condemn John for eating no bread and drinking no wine and then when I come along and throw a big party you damn me as well. So if that's the way it is then I say pass the pot roast and the Cabernet. We're not going to please the finger pointers so let's really give them something to point at!" I'm paraphrasing here...but not by much. This is the moment, it seems to me, when Jesus takes the giant step away from his former teacher and moves into a whole new theological world, a world of grace, a world of hospitality, a world of unconditional love. Here Jesus moves from fasting into feasting.

FEBRUARY 8

Jesus tells the story of the man sowing the seeds. I would stake my theological degree on the fact that's all he did…tell the story. It's evident from the many other times he did exactly that. But frustration with such freedom was discomforting to the early Christians just as it is to us today and so Luke sets about explaining exactly what the parable meant.

Balderdash!

Frederick Buechner once said, "A parable is like a joke, if you have to explain it why tell it?"
Exactly.

FEBRUARY 9

One of the fundamental precepts of my own faith comes in my understanding of who Jesus is. Although it may be troubling to some, I find that the best and most accurate description of the role of Jesus in my life is that he is a window to God for me. In Jesus' life and teachings, in his death, I experience an understanding of what is holy in this world, what is divine in this life. In Jesus' life and teachings, in his death, I am resurrected into a realization that our God is a God of compassion, indeed our God is compassion. His life of love, his willingness to welcome, to forgive, to love those who refused to love him in return, are vivid images of the nature of God for me. His refusal to recant, even when it meant dying a horrific death, is a model and guide for me. It points me to God. It directs me to the kingdom. Such a truth is illuminating as raiment turned dazzling white.

FEBRUARY 10

Christianity is a communal faith. One cannot be a Christian in isolation. Oh you can be a good person. You can do marvelous things for the world and for the future but if you want to claim to be a Christian then you have to be in community. Community is where you are forced to love your enemy. Community is where you have to grapple with whether you will forgive those who have hurt you. Jesus was always ticking people off because they wanted him all to themselves and he wouldn't have it. Community, a healthy community, welcomes both new people and new questions. A Christian community, a healthy Christian community, commits itself to equipping one another to do the work of compassion. This means working for peace and justice among all people. It means protecting and restoring the environment...this is becoming more and more a crucial issue of spirituality. It means reaching out to those Jesus called the least of his sisters and brothers. A progressive Christian community is a community shaped primarily by compassion.

FEBRUARY 11

There was a great theologian in the early part of the 20th century, Rudolph Bultman, who claimed that the salvation of Christianity would come only when we demythologized our stories. I think he was right. We need to recognize that many of our stories and images are often inaccessible to the contemporary thinker. We need to demythologize but then we must remythologize. We must find new images, new words, new stories and symbols to proclaim the eternal truth of God's unconditional love. As disciples of Christ, as believers in that amazing grace, we are being called to find new ways to share the old, old story. Some of this may be painful. It may be difficult to say goodbye to some ancient forms but the problem is real and the call is being made to do just that. We need to be asking ourselves if what we worship is God the infinite source of love or the words and symbols we employ to describe her.

FEBRUARY 12

In the Gospel of John there is a secretive figure who appears on numerous occasions. This person is called by John…"The Beloved Disciple". The beloved disciple shows up in the most interesting places and with very little stretching one can come up with a viable hypothesis that this beloved disciple is Mary Magdalene. Mary Magdalene held a prominent position within the early church, so prominent, in fact, that none of the gospel writers could ignore her. Their readers were well aware of the close relationship she enjoyed with Jesus. For any of the gospel writers to pretend otherwise would be folly. What they could do is downplay her role or, as in the case of Luke, imply something dark about her past. But a close reading of scripture and of other accounts not included in the Bible indicates that this woman was more, much more, than someone standing in the background of the greatest story ever told. Indeed, one tradition from a variety of sources calls Mary Magdalene the "Apostle to the apostles"!

FEBRUARY 13

"The unexamined life is not worth living." Socrates stated some 400 years before the birth of Christ and it is just as true today. Jesus calls us into a changed world with changing issues and changing problems that demand a changing faith unafraid to apply new understandings, new ways of thinking, new ways of expressing our beliefs. A life-changing faith calls us to move bravely and boldly toward a faith-changing life.

FEBRUARY 14

My wife and I celebrated our 38th wedding anniversary this year. I will not speak for her but I can say that our years of loving one another have changed us profoundly. We are not the same people we were 38 years ago. Our willingness to sacrifice for each other, to be faithful to each other, to serve each other, to forgive, accept and love each other, have altered our very being. That, you see, is the nature of love. It is my contention, along with millions of others, that God is love and what that means for me is that God is not just an object of love but a source as well. Over the eons of time, God has been engaged in loving God's creation and we, in faltering ways, have sought to love God in return. Such activity has changed both creation and creator. It has changed as we have sacrificed for each other, been faithful to each other, served each other, forgiven, accepted and loved each other. It has changed our very being, both God and humankind. If God is love then God is changing…expanding, extending, exploding with the grace that we dare to call amazing. This is why the arguments against including certain folk because of their skin color a few years ago or their sexual orientation now is so antithetical to the God revealed not just in Jesus but in that old dialogue with Abraham so long ago. God changes because God is love and love is alive and anything alive changes and grows.

FEBRUARY 15

Although Matthew Fox has been a spiritual guide to me and millions of others, he will tell you that his own spiritual guide was his beloved dog. Much like St. Francis, Matthew believes that animals can be windows to the wonder of life and the myriad gifts of God. Matthew's dog showed him what it meant not just to frolic in creation, accepting each day as a gift and offering thanks by living fully in it, but his dog also taught Matthew the importance of trust and forgiveness, acceptance, even love. Matthew provided his pet with food, a home, companionship. Matthew's dog provided him with loyalty, faithfulness, joy. Now before we diminish this understanding shouldn't we ask ourselves if reading such ramifications into this relationship is no more fanciful than imagining Jesus rocketing up to the heavens or Moses parting the Red Sea? If Matthew and others choose to see such divine traits within their pets and such vision allows them to go deeper into the wonders and mysteries of God, should we not celebrate that understanding rather than ridicule it?

FEBRUARY 16

"Is it I?" asked the disciples. They knew they had the capacity to do evil…and so do we. All of life is a matter of choices and we are called by Jesus to make ours in compassion. Matthew Fox tells of the grandfather who was explaining to his grandson about the two hearts that were beating inside him striving to dominate the other. One is dark and demanding, it is filled with violence and hate. The other is warm and inviting, it is filled with love and hope. The grandson asked which heart would win the battle. The grandfather replied, "The one I feed."

Jesus calls us to feed the heart of compassion that beats inside us all.

FEBRUARY 17

"You will know the truth and the truth will set you free."

I have a friend who does a little turn on that passage. He quotes it this way, "You shall know the truth and the truth will make you weird." Another commentator puts it this way, "You will know the truth and the truth will set you free but first it's going to make you really uncomfortable."

FEBRUARY 18

"Why do we even need the Bible?"

There is a sense in which we don't. Surely we recognize that folk who never had access to this particular collection of theological understandings are not prevented from discovering the truth many of us have discovered in the Bible. It is the truth that at the heart of a meaningful life is compassion. It is the truth that a richness and beauty can be ours when we reach out to others. It is the truth that a wholeness of being comes to those who serve and in such service we discover the divine, we discover God. Now you certainly don't need a book to reach that conclusion. You certainly don't need a religion or a church. You certainly don't need a collection of myths from an ancient culture or selection of sermons from a modern one. You don't need any of that...you can go out and try and figure it out on your own...but why reinvent the wheel? Why not study the writings of those who have gone before to learn what they have learned and discover what they have discovered?

These gifts from the past, carefully studied and selectively used, can be an enormously helpful resource on our journey of faith, throwing light across a path that many have traveled before us, pointing a way for us to follow.

That's what the Bible can do and that's why we call it holy.

FEBRUARY 19

I have such trouble with the feast day of Christ the King. It smacks of a kind of triumphalism that isn't in keeping with the life he led. It smacks of a religion that promises not just a meaningful life but a superiority over any other. I know that isn't the intention but that is how it is often understood. Christ the King evokes images of conquest and domination and such a message can no longer be tolerated in today's troubled world.

But since the church at large has yet to see the wisdom of changing the name, it may be helpful to examine the kind of kingdom over which Jesus is king. "It is not of this world," he tells us. It is not of this world so occupied with numbers, power and prestige. It is a kingdom where the poor are blessed and those who are persecuted for following Jesus are welcomed. It is a world where the standards of success are turned upside down. It is a life that doesn't deny the crucifixion but sees it as a symbol of the enormous power of love, a love that cannot be defeated even by death itself.

FEBRUARY 20

One of the great preachers of the twentieth century, George Buttrick once said, "Those who sit at God's table ought to have the good manners to pass the bread."

FEBRUARY 21

Jesus spoke the truth to those in power and because they reigned in a culture of deceit, they killed him. How many other Christs have been crucified in the last two thousand years?

Each time we forbid the faithful from following their hearts, each time we condemn the question or damn the inquisitive, something precious dies just as surely as Christ died on that cross.

FEBRUARY 22

Despite what we proclaim, the very last thing most of us want is resurrection. We'd much prefer having things just the way they are. No surprises, please. Let's just keep doing things the way we've always done them. We say we want resurrection but what we really want is a little resuscitating of the dead. Same dead old ideas, same dead old ways of thinking and doing, but maybe packaged in a little more trendy way. That's not resurrection. That's not Easter.

FEBRUARY 23

Meister Eckhart, the great Christian mystic of the 15th century said, "What good is it to me if Mary gave birth to the son of God fourteen hundred years ago and I do not also give birth to the son of God in my time and in my culture?" "We are all meant to be mothers of God" he said, "For God is always needing to be born."

FEBRUARY 24

Some Christians claim that the reason we are in the fix we are in is that we have wandered from the fundamentals of the faith, fundamentals, of course, determined by them. These include not just archaic language and symbols, not just a literal understanding of scripture but also a decided bias against science, culture, education and more. If only we can reclaim those strict guidelines we will also reclaim the glories of those ancient days; days that included, inquisitions, crusades, anti-Semitism and other religious triumphs. This, of course, is the same thinking that shapes the Taliban and Osama bin Laden. If only we can recapture what once was. I saw a cartoon this past week that showed Jerry Falwell, Pat Robertson and Osama bin Laden, arm in arm. They were singing: "Give me that old time religion. Give me that old time religion…"

FEBRUARY 25

I believe in me. I believe that I am a person of worth and what's more I believe that you are, too. I believe that I am bound to you and to everyone else in the world by that common value. I believe with Thomas Merton..."What we have to be is what we are." That is, God does not love us more because we act a certain way or believe a certain way or live a certain way. We have value not for what we were or what we hope to become but for who we are. Now. Now. Now.

FEBRUARY 26

I judge the Bible by Jesus. I do not judge Jesus by the Bible. Let that sit a bit and allow me to explain. I am, of course, well aware that it is the Bible that gives us our portrait of Jesus. If it weren't for Matthew, Mark, Luke and John, Christianity might still exist but it wouldn't have much to do with Christ. In the careful study of the life and teachings of Jesus, I believe I have found a guide to the kingdom of God. In the Jesus revealed in those few pages called the gospels, I discover what it means to live a life of meaning, justice and hope. That discovering shapes who I am and who I want to become. It also colors how I view everything else in life, including the rest of the Bible. When I encounter philosophies in the world that work against this model for living that Jesus has given me, I reject them. When I find them in the Bible I don't hesitate to reject them as well. I judge the world by Jesus. I don't allow the world, no matter how powerful, to judge Jesus. I judge the Bible by Jesus. I don't allow the Bible, no matter how holy, to judge Jesus.

FEBRUARY 27

St. Francis, who had a great love of God's creation, wrote this hymn. He understood every living thing as being worthy of God's love and a source of praise.

"All creatures of our God and King, lift up your voice and with us sing: Alleluia, Alleluia!

O burning sun with golden beam and silver moon with softer gleam, O Praise him! O Praise Him!

Alleluia! Alleluia! Alleluia!"

How's that for an upper? And what's more a very different take on how God relates to the world and to humankind. There is little, indeed there is no, sense of our miserable condition, our unworthiness, our wretchedness. Here there is only praise and celebration.

"Dear Mother earth, who day by day unfolds rich blessings on our way. O Praise Him!...

O everyone of tender heart, forgiving others take your part, O Praise Him. Alleluia!

All you who pain and sorrow bear Praise God and lay on him you care. O Praise Him, O Praise Him, Alleluia. Alleluia. Alleluia!"

That theology remains strong to this very day. The Roman Catholic order of Franciscan monks and nuns continue to extol that life affirming conviction in the lives that they lead and the witness they bear.

FEBRUARY 28

"Everyone Welcome" often means "You are invited if you look like us, think like us, act like us and behave like us."

There are churches that are very clear that their welcome extends only so long as you are willing to buy what they're selling. There are some churches that are very clear that their welcome doesn't include women in positions of authority. There are churches that are very clear that their welcome doesn't include the unwashed, the unwell or the disabled. There are churches that make it abundantly clear in a myriad of different ways just how unwelcoming they really are.

MARCH 1

There is a natural process, I believe, of our forgetting and remembering God. We engage in it all the time. When we let our anxiety get the best of us, when we breathlessly race from one appointment to the next, when we fail to cherish each day, when we snap at the people who love us or even the people who don't…we forget God. Lent is a time for remembering God. Lent, with its slightly altered feel, reminds us of God's presence…in rest and renewal, in friendship, in forgiveness, in service, in bread and in wine, in this place, in that world…opportunities all for remembering God.

Think of the very word itself…remembering…re-joining ourselves with the divine, reattaching ourselves to that which is holy. In the story of the Garden of Eden, Adam and Eve are attached to God but as they begin to make choices, they move out, they distance themselves, they begin to forget. It is, as I say, a natural process but a natural process that can separate us from the deep meanings of life. It is a natural process that can distance us from what really matters. And so we need to remember, rejoin, reattach.

Someone asked me this week how they could love God. It was a really good question and it caught me off guard a bit. How do we love God especially if God is not a being out there somewhere, not an object that I can point to? How do I love God?

By remembering. By reattaching myself to that which is divine and I do that not by loving a God out there somewhere but by experiencing God right here…in acts of mercy and kindness, compassion and peace-making. This is how I love God…by experiencing the very things that make for God. I am re-membered.

MARCH 2

When I was a child I knew exactly what Jesus looked like. I knew because I had a portrait of him hanging on my bedroom wall. He had green eyes, light brown hair, a long angular nose and he looked to be well over six feet tall. I can't tell you how surprised I was when he showed up one day short, ugly and reeking of booze.

MARCH 3

It's a funny thing about water. It pretty much goes where it wants to. Oh, we can put in a bowl or dam it in a lake but once it gets out, there's no predicting where it will go. Water is the first thing we normally see when we enter a sanctuary. Water is, often, the very first thing a baby experiences the very first time he or she comes to church. Water shaped the ministry of Jesus when he took a dive in the Jordan for John and the Lord.

Water.

It's such a wonderful symbol of our faith. It washes us. It renews us. It sustains us. Sometimes it picks us up and takes us places we never wished or wanted to go.

MARCH 4

"I didn't know I could believe that!" often means: "I use different symbols and metaphors to describe the God I believe in." Good. That means you are taking your faith seriously and listening not just to what others tell you but to what you believe deep within the depths of your soul. Just because the ancient Israelites or the early Christians described God in a particular way does not mean you must. Just because Luther or Calvin or Pat Robertson describes God in a particular way does not mean you have to. What the New Reformation is trying to do is help all of us find meaningful ways of understanding and describing God, new metaphors, new symbols. We no longer live in a time when sheep and goats are sacrificed to God. We no longer live in a time when the father is the ultimate symbol of authority and power. We no longer live in a time when we think that sickness is caused by demons and women are nothing but chattel. It is long past time for Christianity to enter the modern age and find modern means to assist us on our spiritual journeys.

MARCH 5

When society turns to the church and growls, "Mind your own business", every Christian should sit up and take heed. What is our business? If we believe that the church's only business is a kind of private piety reserved for intimate family discussions or Sunday morning worship then I say with all gravity that we have no understanding of what it means to pick up our cross and follow Jesus. To be a Christian is to commit our life to Jesus. This is unequivocal. There is no compromise. To be a Christian is to place our love of God above everything else...including our family, our society, our country. We who claim to be disciples cannot hide from the commitment we have made to Jesus. How we respond to a crisis reveals what we truly believe.

March 6

Most of us haven't a clue how to really rest. Resting comes only when we fall exhausted into bed at the end of another day of frenetic activity. We jumped into the shower, woke up the kids, gobbled down our breakfast, dressed the children, begged them to eat, raced to daycare, got to work, scheduled a meeting for lunch-time, returned all the phone calls, made a little progress on the proposal, almost finished the report, looked up at the clock, raced off to daycare, slammed some-thing into the oven, hope it wasn't the kids, got them ready for bed, read them a story, begged them to sleep, collapsed on the sofa and fell asleep in front of the TV. And weekends aren't any better. The amount of activity that some of us cram into those precious 48 hours is unbelievable. Between hockey practice and soccer try-outs, grocery shopping and house cleaning, party-going and telephon-ing, Sunday night comes in a blur and we're back where we started on Monday morning.

Re-enter the third commandment. Remember the Sabbath and keep it holy.

In his book, "Sabbath-Restoring the Sacred Rhythm of Rest", Wayne Muller suggests that Sabbath isn't limited to a particular day or time but is very much a way of life. Celebrating Sabbath as it was intended to be celebrated begins with setting aside a day to be different and it invites us to integrate that difference into our daily lives. This is the rhythm that Muller is describing in his book. It can and must be cherished and nurtured if we are to understand the benefits of a healthy spiritual life. This is clearly modeled for us by Jesus. Over and over again, the gospel writers tell us that Jesus went to a lonely place to both rest and reflect on what he intended to do. It was in the wilderness that Jesus had time to rumi-nate on the ramifications of his actions. "The unexamined life is not worth liv-ing" said Socrates 400 years before Jesus lived out that truth and called us to do the same.

MARCH 7

I think of that wonderful scene in Huckleberry Finn that I've thought of so many times. Huck and the runaway slave Jim are floating down the Mississippi river, moving ever closer to freedom for Jim. Huck knows that what he is doing is against the law. He knows that all of society is against him. He knows that the churches in his town and the Christians that were his neighbors would all say that helping a runaway slave is a grave sin against God and yet, and yet, Huck decides he must be true to himself. He must be faithful to his own heart. And if this means he will burn in hell then so be it. It is that dramatic movement from law to grace, from legalism to love. Dare I say…from John the Baptist to Jesus of Nazareth, from fasting to feasting?

MARCH 8

Jack Good's "The Dishonest Church" is an excellent explanation of this ecclesiastical phenomenon some of us are calling the New Reformation. The author attempts to describe the significant differences dividing those Christians who are content with the way things are and want to keep it that way and those Christians who are seeking new ways of expressing their commitment to Jesus. One of the differences the author sees is in how Christians deal with ambiguity. He suggests that there are Christians who are chaos-intolerant and those who are chaos-tolerant. People who are chaos-tolerant don't need to be told exactly what to believe and what not to believe. Chaos-tolerant people are content to see the process through, to recognize that there can be a myriad of ways of understanding problems and approaching solutions. There is no question in my mind that Jesus was chaos-tolerant. His constant challenging of the rules of right order are vivid evidence of that. His welcoming outsiders and those who didn't belong simply underscore my argument.

MARCH 9

"If you love me", Jesus said, "you will keep my commandments." And what commandments are those? Since Jesus was a good Jew, I suspect they had to include the ten given to Moses long before and generally ignored by most of us. From the first to the last, we have found ways to show our kids that those laws don't really matter much. But, truth to tell, we've been doing that since the very beginning of time. There are those other commandments of Jesus that should be giving us pause these days. The ones he taught by the life that he led. The ones that would have us honoring the outsider and welcoming the stranger. The ones that would have us loving our enemy and forgiving our neighbor. Those are the commandments that witness to whether we love Jesus or not. Each time we disparage another human being, each time we act out of violence rather than compassion, each time we respond with hatred instead of charity, each time we shrug our shoulders and say there is nothing we can do, we show the world what we really believe in.

MARCH 10

To be a Progressive Christian means that we recognize that our commitment to the life and teachings of Jesus may put us in difficult situations from time to time. It may demand that we lose rather than win. Give rather than receive. It may mean that we are last rather than first all the time. This could be a very difficult realization for we who live in one of the richest countries in the world.

MARCH 11

What I am suggesting is nothing less than our being open to another Pentecost, another time when the spirit will come and allow us to hear in our own language. And please remember this spirit that came to those gathered in Jerusalem so long ago did not come to keep everything just the way it was. Rather it came and announced an end to the old ways and the beginning of the new. "Young men shall see visions, old men shall dream dreams…" Changes are coming to Christianity. Changes are coming that will threaten its very existence. Changes are coming that will have some people in power ringing their hands and wailing their woes. But a religion that has lost its purpose, a religion that no longer speaks with words and symbols that make sense is a religion that needs another Pentecost where men and women, gay and straight, old and young, rich and poor, third world and first, all of them and all of us will hear the Good News of God's unconditional and amazing love in a language that each of us can understand.

MARCH 12

In Jesus we find a teacher who employs techniques that are not just counter-cultural but are indicative of the kingdom of God.

"Do you want to know what God is like?" Jesus asks, "Well, look around us! Look around and see that this movement includes not just men like me but women and children, rich and poor, clean and unclean, insiders and outsiders. All equal in the sight of God. This is the kingdom of heaven!"

How difficult, even deceitful, it is to claim a hierarchical system as emanating from God when the very one we name our faith after used no such system at all. To this very day the church perpetuates this heresy. Even we Lutherans have been slow to recognize the incongruity. It was less than forty years ago that women were allowed to be Lutheran pastors.

It took us nearly two thousand years to figure out the real story.

MARCH 13

I've always had a rather generous image of God's amazing grace but in the last decade or two it has grown huge. Such a development, as wonderful as it is, is not without its problems. When your understanding of God's love develops at the rate it has for me it can lead you in all kinds of uncomfortable situations. For instance, if you arrive, as I have, at the conclusion that nothing can separate us from the love of God, nothing at all, then you are forced to conclude, as I never grow tired of saying, that God's love encompasses not just those who look like me, or act like me, or worship like me but even those who don't believe as I do, even those who don't accept the theological presuppositions I do, even those who have never heard of Jesus, even those who have rejected Jesus as Lord and Savior…even those are loved and cherished by God. Such a realization forces one to re-examine the very foundations of one's faith. And in that re-examination one must exclude any tenet that denies this wondrous grace. Any tenet, no matter where it comes from. As frightening as it may be I now must reject those self-serving restrictions on God's grace even if they come from the Lutheran confessions, the historic creeds or The Holy Bible itself. I say that carefully but when you live under grace you cannot live cautiously. You are forced to open yourself up to all kinds of new and wonderful ways for experiencing the ever-flowing love of God.

MARCH 14

Somewhere I remember reading that the church is the one place we can go to sing, pray and learn with people we wouldn't want to be friends with. It's the one place where we eat and drink with folk we might never invite over for dinner. Does that sound hypocritical or harsh? I find it wonderfully liberating. As wonderful as all of you certainly are, I simply can't like all of you. And I certainly don't expect all of you to like me. But I am called to love you and, in the name of Christ, you are called to love me. That is the church.

MARCH 15

Do you understand how traditional Christianity has turned its back on creation by forgetting that it is good? One of the most vivid examples of this forgetfulness came a number of years ago when then Secretary of the Interior, James Watt, a born-again Christian and the man charged with caring for creation if you will, announced that since he believed that Jesus would soon come again and all the world would be destroyed, the Department of the Interior's job was severely limited! That is a Christianity that has forgotten its roots! And that is only one example. Christian history is filled with others equally flagrant and disturbing. You see, if you believe that life here really doesn't matter, if you believe that the body is basically unclean, if you believe that the planet is ours to use and abuse any way we want, if you believe that…and much of Christianity certainly does…then you have put the lie to that ancient liturgy that opens up our holy book: "And God saw that it was good, very good."

MARCH 16

The Bible, like all sacred texts, was written to describe a particular understanding of reality. In our case, it begins with the understanding of an ancient religious tradition known today as Judaism. The Hebrew Scriptures or what is often referred to as the Old Testament is the cumulative work of a particular religion's attempt to understand who they are and what life is all about. Christianity emerged out of Judaism with a reinterpretation of some of the Hebrew Scripture to proclaim a new understanding of how God is at work in the world through Jesus. This reinterpretation is found in the second part of our Bible that we call the New Testament or, perhaps better, the Christian Scriptures.

Now there are a number of issues that need to be dealt with before we can even begin to get a grasp of how the Bible, both Hebrew and Christian, should be understood. The first is language. The Bible wasn't written in English, King James' or otherwise. The Hebrew Scripture was written in Hebrew but was translated into the Greek several hundred years before Jesus. So the early Christians used a translation of the original texts to interpret this new understanding of the ancient Hebrew. The New Testament was written in Greek but we have to remember that Jesus' language was Aramaic and although he may have been able to read and write in Greek and/or Hebrew he spoke in a different language than how it was eventually written down. Do you begin to see the problem here? Any one who has traveled to a foreign country knows some of the difficulties around translating what you want to say to someone who doesn't understand a word of what you're saying!

MARCH 17

These are uncomfortable times just as they were uncomfortable in the time of Luther. It takes courage to speak out for what we believe when others tell us we are not only wrong but damned to hell for believing it. But surely that is what it means to be a reformation church. Surely that is what it means to honor the legacy of Martin Luther and all those brave women and men who had the courage to speak out against injustices done in the name of God even, indeed especially, when those injustices are perpetrated by the church.

MARCH 18

Who is a saint? Anyone who brings God near, that's who. A saint is the one who opens the door, pulls up the shade, or flicks on the light and proclaims…"Heeere's God!"

MARCH 19

I checked in the book I have that lists all the Lutheran churches in America. I was interested to see how many congregations call themselves "Christ the King Lutheran Church". Within a few pages I counted 20 of them. On the same pages I counted up how many were called "Christ the Servant Lutheran Church". There were 2. The ratio was ten to one. Of course it's not fair to assume much from this but I suspect that is just about the ratio we could find in all of Christianity regarding how we view the role of Jesus…as king or as servant. Where we fall in that equation makes a big difference in how we understand our faith and how our faith engages the faith of others.

MARCH 20

"Thankyouthankyouthankyou", prays Anne Lamott.

Maybe that is what it means to be a Christian. Maybe it has less to do with believing this creed or accepting that doctrine and everything to do with simply saying thanks. And if that is the case…and there is a very strong case to be made…imagine the possibilities for bridging the religious gaps that separate us. What would happen if instead of highlighting our differences we came together to offer thanks? What would happen if instead of arguing this arcane principle against that arcane thesis, we bowed our heads and said grace?

MARCH 21

Christianity emerged within a world filled with many gods.

There were gods that controlled the weather, gods that ruled the earth, gods that chose your occupation, gods that gave you children, all kinds of gods. And these gods didn't just stay in their celestial homes. They mixed and mingled with the locals. Indeed, their mixing and mingling often resulted in the birth of half-human, half-divine children imbued with the best attributes of both worlds. It was nothing in the days of Biblical writing to have folk wandering our planet who could walk on water, heal the sick, even raise the dead a time or two.

MARCH 22

The fundamental question of Christianity for me is: "Who is Jesus?" For far too long, I believe, the answer has been found in bizarre Christological formulations that have divorced Christ from Jesus. Too often we have been told to worship a Christ that has little if anything in common with Jesus. Can you imagine, for instance, Jesus ever preventing someone from joining him at the table? Can you possibly picture Jesus sending someone away because they didn't completely agree with what he was saying? How about Jesus announcing that it's ok to wage war on another people because of their religion? But that is precisely what has happened in too much of Christianity and, I dare say, that it continues to happen.

MARCH 23

Thanks particularly to George Frederick Handel, most Christians have assumed Isaiah 9:6 ("For unto us a child is born...") was written for them. But, in fact, these powerful words put to beautiful music are spoken by the first prophet Isaiah to King Ahaz of Judah some 730 years before the birth of Jesus. If you are a scholar of Hebrew scriptures you know that Isaiah is foretelling the birth of a child of the royal family who will grow up to protect Jerusalem from Syrian invaders. But because Matthew decided to use the words of Isaiah to validate his understanding of Jesus, we Christians have usurped the sacred writings of another faith tradition, Judaism, and used them for our own purpose.

Ethical problem here? Perhaps, but before we put on sackcloth and ashes, let's remember that Matthew and most of the other writers of our Christian scriptures were faithful Jews who believed they were being faithful to their ancient religious tradition in using their scriptures to justify their new beliefs. Nevertheless, we still have this nagging problem: How do we honor our Jewish brothers and sisters and yet, in effect, tell them that they got it wrong?

One possibility might be to ask ourselves if to be our savior must Jesus be the Jewish messiah? Certainly this was the conviction of those first Christians but even by the end of the first century, Christianity had moved far away from Judaism and begun to establish itself as something very different than its religious parent. Maybe the time has come for us Christians to announce in the boldest of terms that this faith of ours no longer represents a rejection of Judaism but can and must stand independently from its heritage.

MARCH 24

Some Christians seem to pretend that language doesn't matter. They sing the songs and pray the prayers in church using words and symbols that they would quickly reject in their everyday worlds. Such practice creates, I believe, a kind of religious schizophrenia. Worship, spiritual disciplines, theological discussions become nothing more than going through the motions. It is because they can no longer believe the words they are using. Faith becomes empty. Religion becomes a lie. They've kept the bathwater and tossed out the baby. Certainly this is one of the reasons main-line churches are withering up and dying away.

MARCH 25

I've always been interested in the coming of the kingdom but unlike the religious best sellers that describe in graphic detail the end of the world and the impending doom of most of its inhabitants, the coming I'm most interested in is the one that happens every day and most every where. This is the kingdom that, I am convinced, Jesus was pointing out over and over again for his disciples. It is a kingdom that coincides with our world, a kind of parallel universe that we can step in and out of as we wish or sometimes even when we don't wish. "The kingdom of God is among you." Jesus said and I imagine a kind of balancing act between this world and that world. Think of the prayer he taught us all. "Thy kingdom come on earth as it is in heaven." Here. Now. At any moment. Sometimes when we least expect it.

MARCH 26

Take the Bible seriously but not literally. Use your imagination! This is so diffi-cult for so many people. Why oh why did Jesus speak in stories? Surely it was because he wanted his listeners to use their imaginations. Surely it was because he knew that different people approach similar problems in different ways. The wonder of the Bible for me and many others is just when you think you've got it all figured out, just when you're ready to write the rule or proclaim the doctrine, someone comes along to show you something new. Jesus did that over and over and over again. He always shows us something new and calls us to do the same for others. It drove the religious authorities crazy back then and continues to do the same today. Jesus invites imagination not edicts, creativity more than com-mandments. Read the Bible uncritically, at least at first. Don't get caught up in whether this or that could actually happen…enter into it! Live the story first, study it later. To get bogged down in whether this is fact or that is fiction is to run the risk of missing out on what is profoundly true.

MARCH 27

There is more to Christianity than one particular understanding. One might have great faith in the God revealed by St. Francis and less in the God revealed by St. Paul. I don't for a minute believe that we have to swallow it all, hook, line and sinker. I believe that the formation of modern day Christianity is the result of a plethora of theological streams that have, over time, come to form one huge river that we call Christianity. And I am further convinced that I can have faith in that wondrously wide river without having faith in every one of the streams that brought it into being.

MARCH 28

When I served a church in Iowa twenty some years ago, there was a home for developmentally disabled adults only a few blocks away. Every Sunday a busload of these residents would be dropped off for the second service. They would sit in the front two rows and sort of cheer the pastors on. They were especially good at applauding, offering a rousing ovation after what they considered a particularly good prayer or benediction. They would often laugh out loud simply because they were having a great day out of the institution. Sometimes their laughter would be inappropriate but most of the time it just meant they were happy to be there. In any case, this was about the time most Lutheran churches in America were introducing the passing of the peace in the liturgy. Before we receive the bread and wine, the instruments of reconciliation with God, we must be reconciled with one another. And so we turn to our neighbors, embrace in the Lord, and say, "Peace be with you." Well, I cannot tell you what pleasure this little action brought our disabled friends. They would start getting ready many minutes before the actual event, removing their jackets and sweaters in order to hug all the better. It was as if I was announcing the start of a track and field event each time I would say, "Let us share the peace of Christ with our sisters and brothers in Christ." They would come leaping out of their pews, racing around the sanctuary doing their level best to share Christ with everyone in worship. It was disconcerting to more than a few of the folk, I can tell you. Remember I was in Iowa. And in that act of holy chaos, one could witness just how welcoming our congregation really was.

MARCH 29

Islam, as I am slowly coming to know it, is as diverse and varied as Christianity. There are Muslim folk who are convinced they have it all figured out and there are others equally convinced that they don't. I always thought the fact that Christians couldn't get along with each other was an affront to Christ. I suspect Muhammad must feel the same about his own.

In any case, our temptation to present a homogenized version of Islam is as wrongheaded as trying to get a Southern Baptist and a Roman Catholic to agree on the meaning of transubstantiation.

MARCH 30

Everyday I try to set aside some time to do nothing and it often is the most important part of my day. To simply breathe and be aware of my breathing. To live and be aware of my living. To eat a peanut butter sandwich and be aware of the peanut butter sandwich. How can we possibly hope to experience the kingdom of God if we are so busy building our own kingdoms?

MARCH 31

Doubt is my companion and although it has been troublesome at times, I can't think of a better guide for my journey. Doubt is the risk we take to grow in faith. Doubt allows me to push the envelope, to explore places where some would say I shouldn't go. But for me, doubt and faith live side by side. One keeps pushing into the other. Kahil Gibran wrote, "Doubt is pain too lonely to know that faith is his twin brother."

APRIL 1

We have done a great disservice to Peter's legacy by turning him into such a saintly statue. We have robbed ourselves of the opportunity of discovering anew that the kingdom of God comes most often not all wrapped up in a perfect pious package but rough and ready, warts and all. For too long the church has perpetuated an image of sainthood that has less to do with the desire of Jesus and far more with the powers that be. Instead of celebrating the imperfection of men and women like Peter, we have tried desperately to show them without flaw. Christians have, over the centuries been depicted from both within and without the church as a passionless people so afraid of doing anything wrong that we never do anything right. It reminds me of the story of the fellow who decided to go worship at a church known for the excellent and well-ordered, well-planned worship and superb preaching. This visitor was so moved by the sermon that he spontaneously shouted out, "Praise God" at the end of it. The person on his left quickly whispered to him, "We don't praise God in this church." The person on his right then said, "Yes we do but not for three more pages."

APRIL 2

I am drawn to a passage in Paul's letter to the Philippians where he quotes an ancient Christian hymn, "Let the same mind be in you that was in Christ Jesus who, though he was in the form of God, did not regard equality with God as something to be grasped but emptied himself taking the form of a servant..." What did he empty himself of? Could it have been those very opinions and assumptions that all of us make about each other? Could it be that Jesus shed himself of the biases he certainly must have had against our broken race and opened his arms in unconditional love? Is it possible that the love he had for rambunctious Peter or his forgiveness of the adulterous woman or his compassion on little Zaccheus enriched his life and led him to even greater depths of understanding and love? Could this be the kingdom of God that he spoke of so often?

   I dare to believe that such is the case and that Jesus desired it for all of us because he was discovering just how wonderful it was for him. Openness, vulnerability, hospitality...."He emptied himself..." and so must we.

APRIL 3

Although I've never seen it with my own eyes, I'm told that the wooden table that Luther used as his desk still bears an inscription he carved with his own hands. "I am baptized," he wrote in the wood. "I am baptized". Lutherans don't like to admit it but the evidence is pretty clear that our founder suffered from what today would probably be called clinical depression. He was plagued by doubt and despair. Read some of what he wrote while under that dark spell and you'd quickly wish to become a Presbyterian. Which is why he carved the words. "I am baptized". No matter what happens next, no matter how dark my mood, how confused my thoughts, how wrong I am, I am now and forever will be baptized.

APRIL 4

The very word "faith" is problematic. To many folk, faith means believing certain precepts, principles and doctrines…even when they don't make sense or no longer are understood. A young boy was asked what faith was and he replied, "Faith is believing what you know isn't true." And, sadly, many Christians continue to think that way. This is not faith. It is ignorance. It is deception. It is not faith. Do you remember the story of the woman who touched Jesus' robe and was healed of her illness? "If only I but touch his robe I shall be healed," was her thought. Jesus said, "Your faith has made you well." I can't imagine he meant, "Your complete acceptance of the doctrines of Judaism and in particular those passages referring to the Messiah most evident in the writings of the prophet Isaiah have made you well." I think he meant, "Your trust and your love of me has healed you."

APRIL 5

Do you ever wonder why we are so reluctant to talk about our faith? "Forgive me for sounding like a prude but…" "I don't want to come off like a fanatic but…"

What are we so afraid of? Why have we been so reluctant to proclaim our religious faith when it seems so easy to announce our political loyalty? May I suggest that there is a sense that one is rather cheap and the other brings a terrible cost. I have nothing but enormous respect for the men and women who are risking their lives in service to our country. They are putting their lives on the line for a cause that, I assume, they believe in. But surely we must ask ourselves: Why haven't we, who call ourselves Christians, been willing to do the same? The opportunities are everywhere. Are we embarrassed to stand up for the oppressed when someone tells a racist joke at a party? Do we not want to make a scene when confronted with snide and sexist remarks? Do we continue to allow our children's lives to be filled with violence and pornographic images from TV because we don't want to cause a commotion? Do the millions of hungry in this world and the thousands of homeless in this country not merit our attention as followers of the one who was born homeless and poor and died the same? Why, I wonder, haven't we been waving loaves of bread or displaying the cross of Christ the way we now wave the flag? I submit it is because one is really rather easy to do and the other is terribly, terribly hard. This is a crucial time, we have said it before, because we are discovering what we really believe, where we truly put our faith.

APRIL 6

Not too many years ago, I asked my confirmation class to bring in the prayer they said before eating. Some of the kids nodded but many of them indicated that such a request was confusing. "What prayer?" they asked. Over half the kids in that class never said grace. They had no idea that prayer was a part of life outside of church. The simple act of offering thanks before eating is a wonderful way to begin integrating Sabbath into our lives. To take a moment or maybe much longer to savor the pleasure of just being alive is to step into the wilderness, to step out of the rush that refuses to allow us the joy of reflection. Begin your Sabbath journey with prayer, simple savoring of life, gentle gestures of gratitude. Somewhere I read that it is a Jewish custom not to offer petitionary prayers on the Sabbath. We don't focus on our wants in Sabbath time but on our blessings. Spend time each day giving thanks.

APRIL 7

This new Christianity that is taking root in congregations all over the world is profoundly different than the Christianity we were taught as children. It can be found in the tension between a dualistic understanding of the world and a dialectical understanding. That is the difference between either/or and both/and. We live in a time when many folk are fighting vigorously to maintain a dualistic understanding. It's us against them. You're either with us or against us. But the message many of us receive as we study the life and teachings of Jesus is one that is courageous enough to welcome alternative views, different understandings. What matters, many of us believe, is Jesus teaching compassion for others, compassion for the world, compassion for our enemies. That is the central theme of Jesus' teachings. How that is taught is actually irrelevant. It can come from a myriad of ways if compassion is at its heart. It can be found in a myriad of different religions and philosophies. Someone said to me recently, "If Christianity is just about compassion then it is just like any other religion." I said, "Yes!" I heard that yes as affirmation of Jesus' teachings. I suspect my friend heard it very differently.

APRIL 8

I always remember the way my confirmation class was taught so many years ago. A question was offered to which none of us dared answer and then the pastor would confidently read from Martin Luther's Small Catechism…."This means…." and then he would end each answer with "This is most certainly true." Yikes! No ambiguity there! The beauty and benefit of Jesus' style has been lost to many Christians…and, I dare say, to the world.

APRIL 9

Maybe, just maybe, Jesus took that child in his arms not as a symbol of timid acquiescence but rather as an invitation to inquiry. Perhaps, just perhaps, Jesus sees following in the faith as a lively and boisterous spiritual journey that includes all the questions and doubts that come with healthy self-discovery.

APRIL 10

Start with the Aramaic word that gets translated "Father": "Abba". One of the interesting traits of Aramaic is that the sound of the word matters. In a word like "Abba" the very pronunciation is of significance as we probe the depth of its meaning. Abba is often translated as "Daddy" although such nomenclature fails to capture the richness of the intimate relationship implied here. "Abba" Say it. Breathe it in and breathe it out.

APRIL 11

The world is broken, broken in ways that sometimes can feel as if it can never be made whole again.

I began my day as I usually do with coffee and the paper…only something was different…or perhaps, more accurately, I noticed a difference. As I scanned the front section I found that I hesitated only briefly on the stories that focused on the crucial problems facing our world today. Palestine, Iraq, Indonesia. A story of several innocents being killed in a firefight on the Gaza Strip warranted only seconds of my time. A soldier is killed in Iraq and I rush by with merely a glance. More horrifying tales are met with more emotional indifference until by the seventh or eighth page it dawns on me just what I have been doing. I've been trying to pretend that the world isn't broken. I've been trying to protect myself from the harsh realities that most of the world's population has to face everyday. I've been acting as if being a Christian is something I can turn on and off like a water tap. On when things are going well and challenges are small and mostly surmountable and off when the going gets tough and the risks of the faith grow larger.

APRIL 12

Music inspires. It motivates and encourages, it describes and defines, it unites, as well. From the very beginning of time, it seems, music has been a part of the human condition. It is how we tell the stories of our lives…our history and our hopes, our sorrows, our joys, our trials and our triumphs.

I've long been convinced that the kind of hymns we sing in our worship should reflect this rich tradition as well as driving us forward into the future. A new reformation is emerging within Christianity and part of its revelation comes in the hymns that we choose for worship. We are growing ever more reluctant to sing hymns that claim a faith we no longer revere or respond to. Obvious examples would include "Onward Christian Soldiers" or "There is a Fountain Filled With Blood". But even less offensive and certainly long cherished hymns are being carefully examined to see if they still proclaim the message of Christ as we move into the 21st century.

Hymns aren't all about words, of course. A melody may be all that is needed to move us into the kingdom that surrounds us.

Music has power, the power to alter our moods and manipulate our attitudes.

We can all think of examples where music has been used to less than noble effect. But we also can easily remember those songs that have shaped our history in a myriad of positive ways. "We Shall Overcome" and "The Battle Hymn of the Republic" come quickly to my mind. In my own religious heritage, I can recall "A Mighty Fortress" as being one of the great formative hymns of the Lutheran tradition or "Holy, Holy, Holy" as another. But our hymnody, like our theology, is always engaged in the test of relevance. Do the images still mean what they once were intended to mean? Do the symbols still work? Are the metaphors still understood?

James Russell Lowell wrote a hymn back in the middle 1800's that included this line: "New occasions teach new duties, time makes ancient good uncouth." The New Reformation boldly claims that now is a "new occasion" and we Christians are called to distinguish our new duties.

APRIL 13

Over the last twenty years, I have come to realize that my faith is never something to argue over, never something that demands another's acquiescence, never something to force upon others. It is rather something to be lived. It is in my living that I proclaim what I believe. It is in my stumbling, faltering struggle to follow Jesus that I announce to others what matters to me and what matters is God's amazing, unending grace. All the words, all the arguments, all the carefully constructed theological treatises amount to nothing without the witness of my life. To live a life of grace, imperfect as it certainly is, is to announce my belief in a God of all grace, a God who accepts me in my own imperfection and calls me to accept others in theirs...even when that imperfection denies the very God of grace I worship. A friend of mine says that the only thing he is intolerant of is intolerant people. But it is precisely there that God calls him. Not to argue but to love. It is an awesome and often terribly difficult call.

APRIL 14

Not too long ago, someone asked me if I had ever changed my mind. I suspect they were offering a critique on my lack of hesitation to share my opinions. It was a good question and it has stayed with me. My answer is yes, I have changed my mind, significantly, deeply but that change has occurred gradually, gradually as I realize again and again that the kingdom of God is greater than I had previously imagined. Gradually as I come to understand that amazing grace has no limits. Gradually as my eyes are opened to what Jesus realized in his encounter with the Canaanite woman: unconditional love is precisely that. It cannot be contained. It keeps stretching further and further afield.

APRIL 15

Panentheism is the belief that everything in creation is in God. God is not out there somewhere but all around us. Honoring creation allows us to honor God. Defiling creation by the misuse of natural resources, the fouling of our air, the paving of our planet, allowing millions to die of AIDS and millions of others to be innocent victims of politically expedient wars, is to defile God. For those of us who no longer believe in a God up there somewhere listening to our pitiful pleas and self-centered demands, the idea of all of life being God resonates deep within us. It provides a means for holy intimacy with the divine. God isn't distant and removed. God is immediate and present. Surely this is what Jesus meant when he said that the kingdom was in our midst. And if that kingdom is present and now, we Christians should be spending our time and energy seeking to enter into it rather than escape from it.

APRIL 16

Jesus spoke in Aramaic not Greek. We are told that Jesus once said, "It is easier for a camel to go through the eye of a needle than a rich man to enter the kingdom of heaven." As Jack Spong points out, camels don't go through needles...not even teeny-weeny camels. But in Aramaic the word for camel and the word for rope are almost identical. So did Jesus say it is harder for a camel to go through the eye of a needle or a rope to go through the eye of a needle? One is impossible; the other may have a little wiggle room. Or we can deal with the problem of translating Hebrew into Greek when we look at a famous passage from Isaiah that Matthew used in writing about the birth of Jesus. Matthew used the Greek translation of the original Hebrew when he quoted Isaiah 7:14 to describe the miraculous conception of Jesus..."A virgin will conceive and bear a son and his name shall be called Emmanuel." Only in the original Hebrew the word is "almah" which is never understood in Hebrew as virgin but rather a young woman. A whole doctrine was developed around this mistranslation! My point is not to argue against the perpetual virginity of Mary but rather to point out the incredible difficulties inherent in translations.

APRIL 17

I am certain that when Jesus began eating and drinking with tax-collectors and sinners there were many among the religious who were certain he was playing with fire. And, of course, they were right. He was and so must we. We must play with the fire of the Holy Spirit that calls us to move outside the boundaries we have established to keep us in and others out. We must play with the fire of the Holy Spirit that reminds us that we cannot confine God to our way of thinking and our way of believing.

Not too long ago, a United States General declared that Muslims worshipped a false God. I declare that such arrogance is precisely why we need a church that is always reforming. Our doctrine, our creeds, our prejudices and our promises are all false gods in the sense that they cannot capture the God revealed by Jesus. They cannot capture the God of amazing grace, of utter and unconditional love.

APRIL 18

Angels unaware. Isn't that a lovely phrase? You can find it in the 13th chapter of Hebrews. We all know people who bear witness to the reality of a God who is love. They do it in the lives that they lead. Not perfect. Not even pious. But still they are vivid reminders to us of the presence of God. They may not know it but they are windows to God. They are the ones who bring God closer to all of us.

APRIL 19

In a watershed book entitled "The Dishonest Church", author Jack Good examines the devastating effect on congregations that fail to confront the many inherent dishonesties that can plague Christianity. Along with Mr. Good, I think it terribly crucial that we Christians recognize that there is a diversity of opinions within Christianity about how the world is ordered. Many Christians are convinced that there is a nice, neat, divine plan that shapes all that we do or don't do. But some of us believe we live in a world where chaos, not order, reigns.

When, after some terrible tragedy, I hear well-meaning folk claim that God must have a plan to have allowed such horror to occur, I want to throw up. How people can assume such theological trivialities after the Holocaust, after 9/11, after over a 100,000 Sudanese starve to death in the desert, is beyond me and, I believe if we are truly honest, beyond the thoughtful response of any of us.

Of course we want to believe that there is a kind of moral order to the universe. Indeed, there are vast amounts of energy expended by Christian organizations to verify such a reality but in the end their arguments amount to nothing. One random act of evil is all the evidence one really needs to see the fallacy of their reasoning. One innocent child that dies of a rare disease, a wife killed in a hit and run, a grandfather gassed in Auschwitz...how dare we imply that God had a hand in any of it?

Can good come out of evil? Of course! Indeed, fundamental to our understanding of the message of Jesus is the recognition that out of death new life can emerge. But we must move past the thinking that there is a nice neat plan that God has all laid out for us.

APRIL 20

Long ago, back in Iowa, I had the privilege to serve with a great organist named Harry Christenson…which is a great name for a Christian. Harry could drive you crazy with his demand for perfection. He would spend hours and hours working out a particular piece of music until it was done exactly as he intended it to be done. For hours I would sit in my office and hear him go over one measure…over and over again. It drove me batty. But Harry believed his music was a means of saying thanks and he wanted to say thanks in the best of possible ways.

Harry had a little idiosyncrasy that has stayed with me over the years. Every letter he wrote, every memo he typed, every worship bulletin he prepared ended with the phrase, "Thanks be to God". He never failed to include it. And he never failed to include it because Harry lived a life of thanksgiving. Harry actually believed that his talent was truly a gift from God and that it should always be used to glorify God. There wasn't a service that he played where he didn't begin by thanking God. It was an inspiration to me to see this kind of Eucharistic life-style and to reap its benefits, an inspiration and a guide.

APRIL 21

Somewhere along the line, and it wasn't so long ago, we Christians decided that facts were more important than truth. That is, we attempted to justify our theology by employing history. We confused empirical evidence with theological truth. I remember one of the first interviews I ever had with a congregation. We began with nice little chitchat over this and that. We moved on to how I would handle the Sunday School program and when I would teach confirmation and then just as we were getting to like each other, one of the interviewers slapped his hand on the table and said, "All I want to know is this: Do you believe in the bodily resurrection of Jesus?"

All I want to know? How strange, I thought, that my acceptance as a pastor, probably even as a Christian, came down to one historically unverifiable event. How I lived my life, the values I held, the image I had of God were utterly irrelevant and totally subservient to that one question, "Do I believe in the bodily resurrection of Jesus?"

APRIL 22

Just when we convince ourselves that we know God doesn't want women in our pulpits or gays in our pews, God comes to us in competent, compassionate female pastors, in committed Christian men and women. Just when we decide that being a Christian is the only way to please God we read of a Buddhist feeding the hungry or a Muslim reaching out to the poor. God surprises! Isn't that the proclamation of the resurrection? How can we possibly think then that we can write the story of God?

APRIL 23

Let's just spend a little bit of time pondering the impact the Hallelujah Chorus has had on Christian theology.

The chorus is based on several passages from the book of Revelation. Revelation, as you may or may not know, is a decidedly difficult book to discern. It is written in a kind of code that continues to this very day to flummox most biblical scholars. One thing is certain. This is a book that heralds the triumph of Christianity. It was written in a time when Christians were suffering from terrible persecutions and the author seeks to offer a symbol of hope to a besieged people. In just over two hundred years, however, the shoe will be on the other foot and Christianity will become the religion of the realm.

Constantine, the Roman emperor, will declare it so after his famous conversion in 312. Some Christians today look back on that date with despair rather than joy. Christianity, they think, becomes terribly compromised with Constantine and the next 1700 years comprise a confusing and sometimes terribly depressing legacy of Christian domination.

With Constantine, Christianity tastes power and with power comes, we all know, the temptation of corruption. When we listen to the Hallelujah Chorus do we have the responsibility to remember as well the misuses of Christian power? When we thrill to "King of kings and Lord of lords" do we not also need to remember with humility the onslaught brought by the crusades, the horror brought by the inquisition, the failings of the reformation, the systematic attempts over the centuries to wield a power that gave birth to the most horrific of genocidal campaigns?

APRIL 24

What are we Christians to do with symbols that no longer work but continue to permeate our liturgy, our hymnody, our very creeds. I believe a reformation is taking place within Christianity. It may not be as dramatic as posting 95 theses on a Wittenberg door but it will, I am convinced, be just as transforming. It is the growing recognition that the Jesus of history is not necessarily compatible with the Christianity of history.

Recently I had the great privilege to pay homage to one of my greatest heroes, Albert Schweitzer. Sue and I visited his birthplace in Alsace where there is a little museum that records his life and work. Although I certainly haven't read all of his books, I've read many including his great work on the historical Jesus. Schweitzer, of course, left a life of privilege and renown as a scholar and musician to first study and then practice medicine among the poorest of the poor in the heart of Africa. Here was a man who understood that the message of Jesus transcended time and space and was made real in acts of sacrificial love. I believe that he, better than most, understood the concept of a Cosmic Christ that went beyond historical Christianity and into the heart of all humankind. I wrote down one of his sayings that spurs me on in this new reformation: "What has been passing for Christianity during these nineteen centuries (and we, of course, could now say 20 centuries and more) is merely a beginning, full of weaknesses and mistakes, not a full grown Christianity springing from the spirit of Jesus." That spirit of Jesus is captured for me with the image of the Cosmic Christ, the one beyond history, beyond doctrine, beyond religion itself revealing the very essence of God which is, I am certain, love itself.

APRIL 25

I asked some friends this week, "When has the kingdom come for you?" And one of them said, "Each time I breathe." You know, of course, that there is breathing and then there is breathing. One we never notice at all and the other we notice it all. To spend time each day noticing our breathing is to become aware of the beauty of life, the gift of our being, the graciousness of God. It is to welcome the kingdom.

APRIL 26

Sometimes I think that the worst thing that ever happened to our stories of faith is that they were written down. I know how heretical that sounds but it seems to me that once we started putting them onto the parchment we took away their spontaneity, their freshness, their life. It was when we started writing them down that we foolishly thought we had preserved them forever. What we did instead and too often is sucked the life right out of them. Remember please that the Bible writers didn't set out to write the Bible. That is, these were stories and letters, poems and promises, written for a particular people in a particular place and time. No one was thinking: "Boy won't the folk at LOTM be thrilled with this in two thousand years!" A fun and informative way of approaching scripture is to first ask, "What did this mean then?" and then ask "What does this mean now?" The answers can be decidedly and dramatically different but equally true. When Jesus told the story of the Good Samaritan it surely shocked his Jewish listeners with the idea that some scumbag of a Samaritan could possibly be an instrument of God. Who are our scumbags? Who couldn't possibly be an instrument of God for you?

APRIL 27

This may not be a new reformation at all but rather a return to one of the oldest formations of Christianity. It is highly possible that many of the earlier followers of Jesus believed less in what many of us have come to understand as Christianity. There are indications through hymns like the very ancient "O Splendor of the Father's Light" and many others, that some of the early Christians were focused on matters quite different than the matters that seem to consume so many Christians today. Perhaps these early hymn writers based their theology less on human sin and more on God's creative spirit. They seem to have had a more universal theme than the exclusive ugliness that permeates so much of Christianity today. They say Christianity is for the many rather than the believing elite. Compassion, justice, celebration were as important, maybe even more so, than individual salvation. Rather than emphasize obedience and even obsequiousness, there is a real sense of celebration, of creativity, of dancing with God in the cosmic dance.

APRIL 28

A friend told of being in worship back home somewhere and noticing with great pleasure the beautiful bouquet of tulips that decorated the altar. They were yellow tulips gathered together in a spectacular bouquet but in the midst of all the yellow stood one red tulip that drew her attention. She saw it as a symbol of her own struggle to fit into the church. "This is surely a sign from God" she thought. "I really do belong here even if I am a little different." After the service she heard the pastor say, "Those tulips were beautiful but that one red one looked terribly out of place. Get rid of it."

Including others means changing our own identity. Perhaps here is one of the great failures of the church: We have tried to maintain our identity. We have tried to make sure that the rules and regulations that define who we are remain steadfast. We have resisted and continue to resist those elements that would alter who we are. We have welcomed the stranger but we are adamant that the stranger is the one who needs to change rather than us.

APRIL 29

When I read of folk like Jerry Falwell claiming, "I think Muhammad was a terrorist. Jesus set an example of love, as did Moses, I think Muhammad set an opposite example." I wonder what he is basing his conclusion on…certainly not the behavior of Christians and Jews. After all, we Christians managed to mutilate, maim and murder more than a few million in the past two thousand years and the Bible records our Jewish brothers and sisters engaging in some pretty unloving acts as well.

APRIL 30

I think one of the great tragedies of Christianity came as we left our Jewish roots. Born in an age of Greek thinking and Roman power, Christianity quickly developed a split personality, a dualistic way of thinking: flesh vs. spirit, mind vs. body, this world vs. the next. Real healing comes, I think, when we turn away from dualistic thinking and remember shalom, remember the call to be in right relationship with God, with each other, with ourselves. When we compartmentalize we become sick. When we think that the way we conduct our business is separate from the way we worship God, we are sick and in need of healing. When we think that our politics have nothing to do with our faith, we are sick and in need of healing. When we think that the way we treat our enemies has nothing in common with the way we treat our families, we are sick and in need of healing. To be able to integrate all the various aspects of our lives is a healthy goal, a healing strategy.

MAY 1

I welcome you to engage an ancient spiritual practice…that of slowing down. There was a wise monk who said, "Anything worth doing is worth doing slowly." Try this spiritual exercise today. The opportunities are abundant.

-Try doing the dishes slowly.
-Try making the bed slowly.
-Try walking slowly from your car to the office.

See what happens to your soul when you go about life a little slower than before. You will be amazed. The kingdom will come near.

MAY 2

"And Jesus said to them, 'Be not afraid'".

Now I don't know when it happened but somewhere along my spiritual journey I was graced with the revelation that my image of God was so amazing that it encompassed dimensions inconceivable by any of us. Such a realization allowed me the heavenly vision of a God who loves even when not loved back, of a God who welcomes even those who don't believe, of a God who, always and inevitably, accepts you and even me. It is with that understanding that I celebrate these holy words of Jesus…"Don't be afraid." Don't be afraid of new ideas, new ways of understandings, new relationships, new ways of seeing things. Don't be afraid of it. Embrace it. Celebrate it. Welcome it. Because it just may turn out to be God.

MAY 3

In the movie, "O Brother Where Art Thou", there's a great baptism scene. Delmar, Pete and Ulysses escape from a Southern chain-gang and come across a mass baptism down by the river. Delmar decides to be baptized and Ulysses reminds him that being baptized may erase your sins but it doesn't erase the legal records of the great state of Mississippi. Delmar goes ahead and is baptized anyway…rejoicing that he is forgiven of all his sins including the sin of stealing a pig. When Ulysses reminds him that he always denied stealing the pig, Delmar says that he indeed lied but he's been forgiven of that sin, too.

It's a funny scene and it could have us ridiculing the superstition of baptism until very shortly on the three convicts come across an apple pie cooling on a windowsill. They steal it of course but Delmar leaves some money on the sill to pay for the pie. Delmar, you see, hasn't just been forgiven. He's been transformed. Not all the way, maybe but transformed nonetheless.

MAY 4

This is what faith is for me: a trusting that the God revealed by Jesus is worth dedicating my life to. Note that faith for me isn't trusting in other people's notions about God…as valid and helpful as they may be…but rather trusting in God. I trust in God because I have seen through the life and teachings of Jesus that such a God is worthy of my trust, such a God can bring meaning and purpose into my life. I feel no obligation to accept metaphors or symbols that don't lead me deeper into my conviction. Arguing, for instance, over whether God created the universe in six days or how Noah survived the flood or whether Jesus descended into hell does not impact my faith. These are issues that others have found important but I haven't. I have found that in going deep into the teachings of Jesus, a whole new world of wonder and beauty emerge. I trust that world. I have faith in that world.

MAY 5

"What have you to do with us, Jesus?"

Right now this question has particular significance. To pose religious questions upon the conduct and rationale of our government is dangerous. People will question our loyalty. To wave a Christian question mark instead of an American flag right now seems a most un-patriotic thing to do. I find myself hesitant to apply the gospel critique to this situation in Iraq when American men and women are risking their lives over there. But surely that is precisely what out government and military leaders are hoping. Don't question, just support. Put aside all your religious ambiguity and pick up a flag. After all, what have you to do with us, Jesus?

MAY 6

In certain orthodox Jewish traditions, making love on the Sabbath is a requirement. How's that for a commandment? I bet the evangelism program would really take off if Christians promoted that one! But Sabbath is precisely about savoring the pleasures of creation. Where do we think the traditional Sunday afternoon feast came from? It was this identification of Sabbath and pleasure. It was this remembering of the riches that God desires for us.

MAY 7

Why do we have to be better than other religions? Why does Christianity have to be the winner and others the losers? Why can't we all win? I believe we can. I believe that happens when we move from fasting to feasting, when we move from a faith about Jesus to the faith of Jesus, a faith that was centered not on blood sacrifice or physical resurrection but on compassion, on grace, on the unconditional love revealed over and over again by Jesus.

MAY 8

There is a wonderful Taoist tale that goes…

There once was a Chinese Farmer. One day the gate to the corral is left open and his horse runs away. The neighbors come to comfort him. "How terrible that your horse has run away…" The farmer replies: "Maybe it's good; maybe it's bad; it is too soon to tell yet."

A few days later the horse returns to the corral bringing a whole herd of wild horses with him. The neighbors come to celebrate. "How wonderful that now you have an entire herd of horses!" The farmer replies: "Maybe it's good; maybe it's bad; it is too soon to tell yet."

A few days later the farmer's son begins training one of the new wild horses. He is thrown from the horse and breaks both his legs. The neighbors come to comfort the farmer.

"How terrible that your son has been injured this way, now he won't be able to help you in the fields." The farmer replies: "Maybe it's good; maybe it's bad; it is too soon to tell yet."

A few days later the Emperor's troops march through the village conscripting all the able young men in the village to go to war. The farmer's son is left behind because his legs are not healed. The neighbors come to celebrate and the farmer replies…

MAY 9

We all know the story of Thomas dubbed for all eternity as "Doubting Thomas" and ridiculed from far too many pulpits for far too many years. I've made no secret that Thomas has provided more counsel to me than all the other disciples combined. I agree with Tennyson when he wrote his famous line, "There is more faith in honest doubt than in half the creeds."

MAY 10

Imagine, if you will, some task that you do frequently. See yourself engaged in it. Slow it down. Watch yourself take the time it deserves. Are you taking out the trash? Slow it down. Remember the good meals whose remnants are now being discarded. What a blessing. Making your bed? Slow down. Offer a prayer of gratitude for a good night's rest or the presence of another.

MAY 11

I am certainly aware that there are some who would suggest that Christianity is a refuge from the problems of the world. Many of these folk would prefer that troubling issues be left out there, beyond the doors. Some would even see worship as a kind of escape from the harsh realities of these changing, tumultuous times. It is certainly understandable. It is certainly what many churches have chosen to do. But it is just as certainly not reflective of the life and teachings of Jesus. I find it both fascinating and deeply discouraging that one of the institutions most resistant to resurrection or even reformation is the church.

MAY 12

There really are few places where we sing as a community. The ballpark, I suppose, or campfires, on occasion, and here in church. Singing brings us together. It unites us in a single song no matter how well or poorly it is sung. For those of you who have only felt comfortable singing in the shower but never in church, let me suggest you try just mouthing the words. Pretend your Luciano Pavarotti and just sing along *sans voce*. I promise you it can serve as a wonderful way of entering into the life of the song. The spiritual journey is all about participation even if you have to pretend. No one can sit on the sidelines and still follow Jesus.

Lest we sound too judgmental here, the only point I'm trying to make is how singing is such a unifying force. It can transcend the petty differences that too often divide us…especially, perhaps, in the church. Ever been to a rock concert? Do the folk just sit in their seats and quietly listen? Of course not! Everyone is up and singing along! There is this one incredible force of unity binding everyone together. That is what hymnody can do as well.

MAY 13

Are there ways of experiencing grace outside of Christianity? Are there ways for understanding that Christ goes with those who do not use that name? For me, captured as I am by that radical image of a gracious God, I must confess, yes. Such a confession leads me ever onward into often forbidden, always exciting territory. Such a confession alters my life even as it alters my faith.

I went back and read the first sermon I ever preached at the church I now serve, over twenty years ago. In it I spoke of surprise, of the need to be open to the surprising ways of God. Maybe I haven't changed that much because I still would say the very same thing today. Because that is the way grace always operates…surprising us in wild and wonderful ways. Anytime we foolishly try to limit the power of God by arbitrarily deciding who is worthy for grace and who is not, we have turned our backs on the God who surprises. We have turned our backs on Christ. We have turned back toward that old time religion that forgot about grace and was reminded by Jesus but then forgot about it again and was reminded by Augustine but forgot about it again and was reminded by Luther and forgot about it again and was reminded by Desmond Tutu, Martin Luther King, the Dalai Llama, Mother Teresa, Thich Nhat Hahn, and countless others willing to live life-changing faiths and faith changing lives…and still we forget and still we must be reminded.

MAY 14

"Extra Ecclesiam Nulla Salus." Has a certain ring to it, doesn't it? Too bad it is one of the most offensive church doctrines ever conceived. Literally translated: "There is no salvation outside the church." "Extra Ecclesiam Nulla Salus". It has been used and abused over the past ten centuries against any who might find themselves questioning any minor tenet of the faith. Any theological inquiry, any religious questioning that pushes one toward the borders of the church is squashed immediately and irrevocably by this ancient edict. And don't think for a moment that just because this doctrine emerged out of the Roman Catholic Church it is limited to their own particular form of arrogance. Nearly all of Christianity has employed much the same theory in varying forms. "Unless you believe and are baptized." some would say. "You must be born again." say others. On and on goes the list of exclusions that ultimately lead to those chilling words: "Extra Ecclesiam Nulla Salus."

It is ridiculous, of course. The very thought that we somehow control the work and will of God is the height of blasphemy and the church, both Catholic and Protestant, should hang its head in shame. The world, of course, has moved blithely on, amused, I suspect, by our arrogance. Like Chicken Little, the church has little credibility in a complex world that demands imaginative new solutions instead of relying on ancient and ridiculous worldviews.

MAY 15

It shouldn't shock you when I say that traditional Christianity is dying if not already dead. A religion that sees the world as basically evil and deserving of punishment is a religion that is of little help to millions starving to death and millions of others living under oppressive regimes and millions of others who are illiterate and millions of others who are so envious and angry when they witness what we in the West have done to the planet that they are willing to believe the lies their own religious and political leaders tell them. Christianity needs to return to its true roots, to the belief that creation is worthy of our love and devotion, that every member of this planet from the amoeba in the microscope, to the president in the White House, to the dog in our yard, to the oxygen molecule in the atmosphere, is deserving of our love and respect.

This is what salvation means to me. It has really nothing to do with Jesus being sacrificed for my being sinful and unclean. It has everything to do with his teaching me to honor creation and to live in compassion.

MAY 16

The Hebrew Scripture emerged out of a tumultuous time of tribal warfare. Armies fought horrific battles each claiming, as we do today, that God or the gods are on one particular side. We have the writings of one of these groups. It is understandable that God is on the side of these particular authors. Just as Allah is on the side of Islam, God or Yahweh is on the side of Judaism or Christianity depending on your particular perspective. And because God is on our side, all kinds of actions, seemly and unseemly, can be justified, everything from the murder of innocent women and children to the eternal damnation of non-believers. It is that kind of justification that most of us find repulsive and yet we wonder how we can respond when people use the Bible to validate their views.

We can, and indeed we must, try and peel away the layers of translation and cultural interpretation that can prevent us from seeing the deeper truths of scripture. For Christians, that means carefully studying the records of Jesus, his life and teachings, to get to the heart of what it means to be his disciples. And for some of us Christians, this careful study has led us to the conviction that there are parts of the Bible that are not in keeping with Jesus' teachings. We must decide what is more important: The teachings of Jesus or the Bible.

MAY 17

We have confused our metaphors for reality, our similes for certainty. The healthy church constantly reminds itself of such a danger. The healthy church constantly remains vigilant against false gods; even when those false gods seem so, well, godly.

I believe we are in the midst of a new reformation. Our reformation heirs will read of this time in their history books and recognize that in the early years of the 21st century, the church was in need of change and that there were those within the church who so loved the church and were so desirous of reforming the church that they were willing to risk censure, condemnation and worse. May we be those people. May we be that church.

MAY 18

I've known many saints. One I recall was Anna Powers. She was dying, at least she was convinced she was. She looked pretty healthy to me considering she was 84 or so but every time I paid a call on her in her little apartment she was convinced that today was the day she was going to die. "This is it, Pastor!" she would tell me and then break into the biggest smile imaginable as she imagined what the door of death was about to bring. "I'm going to be with Jesus!" she'd sing and I always hesitated a bit before trying to convince her that she didn't look much like she was going to die to me.

I'll bet I visited that lady 50 times in the three and a half years we lived in Iowa and 48 of those times she was convinced it would be my last visit. She finally did talk God into taking her but that was only a number of years after I had moved to Colorado.

Anna was an angel unaware. Every Sunday, without fail and no matter how close she felt to death's inevitable door, old Anna would be sitting in worship in the same spot she had sat for some 70 years and always looking up at me with an encouraging smile and a how do you do. Talk about a symbol of faithfulness! What a marvelous witness she was to me of the constancy of love, of God's ever presence. I don't think she agreed with much that I ever said. She was definitely of the old school but we were family, brother and sister in Christ, and that alone was enough to spend each Sunday morning smiling back at me from her favorite pew.

MAY 19

No matter how hard you try you cannot go against what your heart is telling you. You can sing louder than anyone else, you can pray more fervently, you can memorize the creeds backwards and forwards but if, in the depth of your soul, you cannot accept as fact what you know to be false, you won't.

MAY 20

I have just returned from a soul walk.

Such activity is engaged not for its physical benefits but solely for the…uh, soul.

Now I have always been one who loved exercise and for as long as I can remember I have taken reasonably good care of my body but my morning or evening constitutionals are experienced not primarily for good physical health but for the honing of my spiritual well-being.

A soul walk, you see, is taken without any extra paraphernalia. Perhaps a nice walking hat but certainly no Walkman or day-glo shorts or $200 Michael Jordan walking shoes.

You should be able to begin a soul walk without a moment's hesitation. Simply grab a jacket and head out the door. All those other accoutrements are the very antithesis of what a soul walk is meant to be.

While engaged in soul walking, one should let the mind simply relax. Soul walks are not undertaken in order to solve life's problems, resolve difficult situations or decide future activities. Soul walks are simply for walking.

MAY 21

I have no doubt that Paul had a profound experience of the resurrected Christ while walking toward Damascus. His experience is so powerful that he interrupts his life's calling and changes his professional direction. He tells of his experience to others, writes passion-filled letters to even more. In fact, he shapes the very foundation of Christianity. All of which I honor and admire. But can we not disagree about some of his conclusions? Can we not critique some of his assumptions? I can and I do. I honor his experience while differing over some of his explanations.

MAY 22

Christianity is at a crossroads and that is a pun that is very much intended. We are at a decision point where we must choose between the faith of Jesus and a faith about Jesus. Too much of our past has been a desperate attempt to develop a faith about Jesus. We have come up with a story that, I believe, hasn't much to do with the stories Jesus told. We have been captivated by a plot that has us thinking we've somehow managed to manage God. We determine who is in and who is out. We decide who will be saved and who will not. All of this antithetical to the way Jesus lived. All of this the opposite of what Jesus taught.

MAY 23

Over the years and in a troubling, curious, way, I've come, more and more, to dread being identified as a Christian. Of course, I am proud to be aligned with Christ but the truth of the matter is there is such a divergence of definitions of what it means to be Christian, I'm not so sure the term has any real meaning any more. If being a Christian means that I believe others who walk a different religious path than I are damned by God, then I'm not a Christian. If being a Christian means that I must drape a flag over the cross and subvert the teachings of Jesus to the demands of the state, then I'm not a Christian. If being a Christian means I must turn off my brain, shut my mouth and accept as fact what I know to be false, then I'm not a Christian. But if being a Christian means that I commit my life to humbly struggling to follow Jesus, then count me in.

MAY 24

Eighteen times in Matthew, Jesus invokes the word "blessed" and eighteen times we get a very different message than the one we are used to. To be blessed in the eyes of Jesus is to recognize the God we worship is a God who favors the outcast, the poor, the weak, the hungry and the persecuted. To be blessed by the God revealed by Jesus is to welcome the stranger, to reach out to the lonely, to love our enemy. Is this the blessing we want when we sing "God Bless America?"

MAY 25

I've long admired the boldness of some cultures in naming their children. We white folk seem to be stuck with serviceable if uninspiring nomenclature. Richard. Susan. Nice names, I suppose, but certainly less than imaginative. But take the practice of some of our Hispanic brothers and sisters…Jesus, for instance. Now that's a name you could be proud of. We hesitant westerners get close but are never quite bold enough to go all the way. We have Paul and Mary, we have Matthew and Luke, but Jesus? Just too close for comfort maybe? Too much of a reminder, perhaps? One of my favorite names is Emmanuel. It is pretty popular with just about everybody but us. It means "God with us". It means the kingdom isn't just coming. It means the kingdom is right now. "Kingdom" is crying in his crib. "Kingdom" just walked in after her first drive. "Kingdom" is playing in the back yard. "Kingdom" is walking down the aisle. The kingdom comes. Now. Here.

MAY 26

In the time of Jesus, the way to get right with God, to be saved, if you will, was to be made pure. And purity came in the ritual acts of purification performed at the Temple and in Jerusalem. You know the story. Once a year you went to the Temple paid a priest to slaughter an animal in order to appease an angry God. The size and cost of the animal was dependent on the size of one's sins. Some folk might only have needed a mouse to carry their sins away. Some of us might need something a little bigger. Looking around this room and thinking about my own situation, one might wonder if there were any elephants waiting in the wings. In any case, that was the deal. Over the course of the year you got a little sinful, a little impure and you paid a priest to put in a good word and a dead animal and, voila! you were right with God. You were saved....at least until the next impure act or thought. It was, as you might expect, a pretty good deal for everyone concerned especially the priests. How God felt about the whole business, I'm not so sure.

We do know how John the Baptist felt. He thought it was a crock...especially the part about the priests. So he set up shop in the Jordan River and let people know that they didn't have to head off to Jerusalem but could take care of everything right there in the water. Now it's important to note here that John still felt that the folk were impure and needed to get right with God. It was just that he would do it for free and with water instead of blood. One could assume this pleased most of the people and certainly all of the animals.

MAY 27

Sometimes, and this can be a terribly difficult thing to understand let alone accept, sometimes the miracle that occurs may not be the one that we pray for. Sometimes the miracle is that the parents manage to keep their marriage together after the terrible strain the death of a child can bring. The miracle may be that their friends and family will continue to surround them with their love and affection weeks, months, years, after the death of their dear child. Sometimes the miracle comes in ways that we can never imagine.

MAY 28

We called him Opa and even on Christmas he would spend most of his day in the basement library of his house reading whatever it is old, retired German Lutheran pastors read in their basements. It seemed to me an incredible library although most of the books were in a foreign language and almost all of them were about theology. Nevertheless, I loved just sitting among them in the dank and dark of that basement. And so on that particular Christmas Day, I snuck down the stairs and sat on the bottom step watching my Opa read and pretty much minding my own business.

After a while, he looked over at me from his desk and, without saying a word, motioned me to come over. I can't remember for sure if he smiled, but I do know that I felt more like I was approaching the King of England than my own grandfather. He stared at me for a while and then asked me my name. This certainly confirmed my conviction that he hadn't a real firm grasp on precisely who I was. But then he surprised me by reaching up above his desk onto a shelf of books and taking down a bright yellow volume. Without so much as a whisper, he opened up the book and on the inside front cover, where his own name was written, he wrote with a fountain pen, "Lawfully transferred to "Richard James Mayfield, Christmas, 1955." He waited a moment for the ink to dry and then he closed the book, handed it to me and went back to his own reading.

I backed out of the basement and half way up the stairs. I marveled at the wonder of it all. I still do. It may be just wishful thinking or sloppy sentimentality but I've always thought, even back in 1955, that my grandfather was trying to tell me that I mattered to him. Even if he had a little difficulty remembering just precisely who I was and which of his own children I belonged to, he wanted me to know that I mattered to him. There is more than a little of the holy in that. There is more than a little of God.

MAY 29

One of my most important mentors has been Thich Nhat Hahn. Once he reflected that most folk think walking on water or in thin air is a miracle. But a real miracle for Thich is not to walk on either water or thin air but to walk on the earth. Every day, he says, we are engaged in a miracle which we don't even recognize: a blue sky, white clouds, green leaves, the black curious eyes of a child, our own two eyes. All is a miracle.

MAY 30

There are no birth stories of Jesus in Mark as you find in Matthew and Luke. What may surprise some of you is that there are also no resurrection appearances of Jesus in this gospel. It ends with an empty tomb and some very surprised ladies. Indeed, the last words of this rapid fire gospel that demands so much are haunting. Mary Magdalene and another woman race away from the empty tomb with fear and trembling because Mark says in describing them and perhaps all of us, "they were afraid." Afraid of what? Didn't they know all the wonderful things that were going to happen to Christianity? Didn't they know how we would become intimately intertwined with the rise of western civilization? Didn't they know that wars would be fought, people would be colonized, political systems would be developed all invoking the name of Jesus? Didn't they know how the church would too often turn this awesome, sometimes terrifying story into a nice neat package for personal success?

No wonder they were frightened.

MAY 31

I remember one night a number of years ago. I awoke with the startling realization that I didn't believe in God. It was very clear, very certain. There was no God. It was the opposite of a born-again experience. It was more like a dead again experience. And then just as quickly as it came, it passed away. But it left me stunned, shaken and wondering. What do I believe? I lay there for the rest of the night and pondered the peculiarities of my faith. I knew I didn't believe in the God many Christians seemed to put their faith in. I knew that my experience with the divine was based more on hope than on certainty. I knew that the life that I was leading, faltering and failure-filled as it was, still brought me satisfaction and meaning. I knew, at least for now, this is my Christian journey. This is what marks my faith. I have not seen and yet I believe.

JUNE 1

Here's another very simple discipline with immediate rewards. Close your eyes right now and make a little half-smile. Can you feel what is happening? There is a physiological change that occurs in our entire being by just shaping our mouths in a little half-smile. Thich Nhat Hahn, the wise Buddhist monk, invites us to use the half-smile in a myriad of ways…when you wake up, while listening to music, when your feeling a bit irritated…maybe at the length of a particular sermon…give yourself a half-smile and welcome the change, enjoy the experience, enter the kingdom.

June 2

A wonderful way of acknowledging the surprising presence of God can be found in a little religious practice passed on by our Hindu brothers and sisters. It is a greeting centered on the word "Namaste". It means literally: "I bow to you." but it has come to mean something more like: "The spirit in me acknowledges the spirit in you." Hands are placed over the heart and there is a gentle bow. It is a new way, I believe, of sharing the peace of Christ with others. I would encourage you to try it today. Greet a friend or a lover, the clerk at the market, the child at the door with that gentle, holy word: "Namaste".

JUNE 3

Do you ever wonder why such good ideas come to us while standing in the shower? Maybe the church should be encouraging people to wash more and worship less?

JUNE 4

"I don't believe in God."

Often I respond by saying: "Tell me about this God you don't believe in because I probably don't believe in that God either." Occasionally this initiates a lively discussion that can plumb the depths of theology. So much of Christianity has been twisted and perverted by men (and women…but particularly men) seeking to make their metaphors the standards for everyone. Examples are abundant. Stories from the Bible of God slaying thousands including women and children are clearly not based on historical evidence but theological assumption. In the New Testament, attempts to define God are everywhere starting with virgin births and ending with spectacular judgment days. Are these the parameters of faith? Not for me. Faith for me is this deep, profound desire to trust that the life and teachings of Jesus are the path to wholeness for me. On my own journey I will discover the words and symbols that serve me well. I may even share some of them with you but because they work for me does not mean that they will work for you. You need to find your own. We turn to those who have gone before us for guidance. We look to those who are traveling with us, but we are not bound to their understanding. This is a journey each of us must make. No one can do it for us.

JUNE 5

In the Gospel of Mark the very first recognition of who Jesus is comes from an evil spirit. Could it be that Mark is announcing what God surely knows…that it is the evil spirits of the world that are most afraid of the power of love? They know, like no others, what can happen when the gospel of God's forgiveness and grace is unleashed. Lives are changed, the sick are healed, the poor are cared for, the hungry are fed. Is it any wonder the demon wants Jesus to mind his own business? Such love can put the demons of this world out of business!

JUNE 6

Re-membering. Putting back together what has grown apart. That is what we are doing by taking Sabbath time. And how disjointed we have become! Families that never sit down together to eat but grab what they can on the run. Couples who haven't stopped to look into each other's eyes in days or months or years. Folk like me or maybe like you who haven't paused to ponder the reason why we're racing off to another appointment. Re-membering. Coming back to where we began. "Blessed are the children" Jesus said and I suspect some of the reason had something to do with their ability to experience sheer joy, the simple pleasure of simply being.

JUNE 7

Please know that these thoughts are deemed heretical by some and even evil by some others. Last week a fellow came up to me during the passing of the peace and berated me for preaching heresy. But it is heresy only to those who think they have a lock on the truth and God in a box. The New Reformation is seeking to reclaim the spirit of Martin Luther who had the courage to ask questions, seek alternatives, suggest new options. Surely we who are heirs to that spirit should be willing, indeed eager, to do the same.

JUNE 8

From Martin Buber…

"My grandfather was lame. Once they asked him to tell a story about his teacher. And he related how his teacher used to hop and dance while he prayed. My grandfather rose as he spoke, and he was so swept away by his story that he began to hop and dance to show how the master had done. From that hour he was cured of his lameness.

JUNE 9

"Now Jesus did many other signs in the presence of his disciples which are not written in this book. But these are written so that you may come to believe that Jesus is the Messiah, the Son of God, and that through believing you may have life in his name." Sounds like the final paragraph to me. And what's more, that verse that began it: "Now Jesus did many other signs which are not written in this book…" is about as intriguing a sentence that you could find in all of scripture. "Many other signs…not written in this book…" Like what? C'mon John you can't tease me like that and leave me hanging! What other signs did Jesus do?

JUNE 10

Did Jesus teach us the doctrine of the trinity or historicity of the virgin birth? No. Did Jesus teach us the Apostle's Creed or the Augsburg Confession? No again. Jesus didn't seem to spend much time teaching doctrines, no matter how holy we now deem them. Jesus was a rabbi and like all good rabbis he taught by example. It is a curious fact that the Judaism of Jesus' day and, I believe, even the Judaism of today, isn't all that concerned with what someone believes but rather what someone does. This can be disconcerting to many Christians who claim it is all about believing certain precepts but it wasn't for Jesus and it isn't for his descendents in Judaism. Indeed, there is a famous story of Rabbi Hillel who is approached by some fellows who say they will become Jews if he can teach them all about Judaism while standing on one foot. The good rabbi complies, lifting up his foot and saying, "Don't do to others what you wouldn't want them to do to you. All the rest of scripture is commentary on that." And he put down his foot.

Jesus, you may remember, said much the same thing. We call it "The Golden Rule".

JUNE 11

There is an old word that has gotten a kind of bad rap over the years. The word is repent. It is usually associated with a wild-eyed evangelist screaming from a street corner but it was probably a word associated more with Jesus than many of us would like to believe. Repent, as it is used in the New Testament, really means to turn around, to change direction. Although it has been associated with hell fire and eternal damnation, it might be better understood as a form of encouragement. Jesus saw the world's brokenness. Jesus saw the power that obsessed some people and oppressed others. Jesus saw the hurt that was caused when the few had much and the many very little. Jesus saw all this and called on the world to repent, to change direction, to discover that the good life wasn't found in how much money you had or status you obtained but in something very different indeed, something that demanded repentance, a change of direction, a change of heart.

JUNE 12

I suppose no part of Christian worship is more controversial than the selection of our hymns. Congregations have split over the kind of music that is played and sung. We are reluctant to change. We like things the way they've always been. But following Jesus into the 21st century demands that we change. It demands that we take into consideration the advancement in science, technology, race relations, political understandings and more, so much more, that make up life in 2004. It seems to me the motto for we Christians should be something along the line that we "honor the past and welcome the future."

JUNE 13

A woman wrote me afraid that she was losing her faith. As I read her letter I became more and more convinced that what she was losing was belief in a graceless religion that wielded power with threats of exclusion and damnation. I wrote her back to tell her that I hoped she was losing her faith but to take heart because she was discovering grace and it was about to change her life which meant it was about to change her faith which meant it was about to change her life which meant it was about to change her faith.

JUNE 14

Just what does it mean to be saved? Our word for salvation comes out of the root: "to be made whole." We are saved when we are made whole. This, I am convinced, is how Jesus understood salvation…as the emergence of our true selves, the unifying of our body, mind and soul. That salvation came to be understood as a kind of insurance policy for the great bye and bye shows how far we have moved from the life and teachings of Jesus to our own wishful thinking. This week I received another one of "those" letters. You know the ones I mean. They generally consign you to the very lowest rungs of Hell for disagreeing with their theology and then sign the epistle: "In Christ's Love." Why are the nastiest letters I receive always signed: "In Christ's Love"? They don't have anything to do with Christ's love! They are written by folk who have turned salvation into a personal thing, a "me and Jesus" thing. Like the very indulgences Luther condemned, salvation becomes nothing more than something you buy only now instead of using coin one uses doctrine. We buy off God with our belief. We buy our salvation with our faith.

But Jesus proclaimed that salvation couldn't be sold, it could only be given away. In his call to service, in his welcome of the outsider, in his forgiveness of those who had hurt him, Jesus images a world of salvation, a world of wholeness. It comes in our relationships with others; it comes as we open ourselves to others, become vulnerable to others. Salvation demands others.

JUNE 15

It is compassion that is at the heart of any theology that truly seeks to honor Jesus. Compassion means, quite literally, the sharing of hearts. To be compassionate is to seek to understand another. It is to try and find ways of relating to every living thing. It is to enter into the kingdom. It is to live with God. When we condemn others for not believing as we do, or when we blithely go about our business with no concern for the environment we live in, or when we bully others into submission, we turn our backs on compassion, we turn our backs on Christ, we turn our backs on God.

JUNE 16

So much of Biblical interpretation comes from the lens we use to read it. Matthew used the lens of Judaism to understand Jesus. That is why in the Gospel of Matthew, Jesus is analogous to a new Moses…who comes out of Egypt and goes up on a mountain to teach and fulfills Hebrew prophesy over and over again. And that is why Luke has Jesus as a much more universal figure who reaches out way beyond Judaism to the far corners of the world. So much depends on the lens we use.

A Palestinian Christian understands the Bible in some decidedly different ways because of his own experience, his own lens. A Palestinian friend spoke of the story in the Hebrew Scripture of Joshua defeating the Amorites. Joshua slaughters every living being in every town he conquers…from the king to his last innocent subject. Those people, he told me, were his ancestors. Could he, as a Christian, actually believe that his God blessed this act of genocide just because it was in the Bible?

JUNE 17

The word Bible comes from the Greek "tab biblia" which means: The books.
Note that. The books…plural. One of the first misunderstandings surrounding
biblical scholarship is the very title we give to this collection of sacred writings.
We've all heard the Bible referred to as "The Good Book" as if it were a singular
work by one author that has a nice, neat plot with a beginning, middle and end.
Wrong! The Bible is a collection of writings by a variety of authors from a wide
range of different times and places. To think of this as a singular work is to make
a fundamental mistake in biblical scholarship. It is also to deny yourself the richness that a deeper look into the Bible can offer.

JUNE 18

Robert Louis Stevenson once wrote, "The saints are the sinners who keep on going." That's a comforting thought for me. In fact, I am convinced that is why Jesus said, "Blessed are those who mourn for they shall be comforted." Sainthood is bestowed upon those pilgrims who know that life isn't a bowl of cherries just because you are a Christian. There are times of sadness and pain so saints cherish every moment of life as a gift from God.

Saints understand that God can be discovered in both the highs and the lows of life. Sainthood comes when we embrace all of life instead of trying to hide from it. In other words, saints live in that tension that exists for all of us between good and evil, right and wrong, laughter and tears. It is in that tension that God is discovered. Plugging along, day after day, we encounter the God who never abandons us and always reminds us of the power of love.

I remember St. Augustine who most humanly offered this famous prayer, "Give me chastity Lord…but not just yet." The power of God comes in the reminder that others have struggled as we struggle now. Are you remembering someone now who brought you nearer to God by their own celebration of life? Close your eyes and see them again and thank God for this angel unaware.

JUNE 19

One of the problems of Christianity is the emphasis on belief. I think we've turned a beautiful way of life into nothing more than a loyalty oath. It's not for nothing that the earliest Christians were called "The Way".

What Jesus taught was not systematic theology; it was not a nice, neat and ordered class on Christian doctrine. Jesus didn't demand we acquiesce to a kind of anti-progressive, anti-scientific worldview. Jesus lived out his faith, he acted on his assumptions, and in so doing he revealed what he believed. Jesus believed in the power of compassion and he lived out that belief by being compassionate.

All the books, all the classes, all the degrees after our names, ultimately have nothing to do with the teachings of Jesus if they aren't accompanied by compassionate action. It is compassionate action that unites us to Jesus…not doctrine, not creeds, not even Christianity itself. Without compassion they are nothing more than semi-interesting historical documents.

JUNE 20

Although I haven't attended a great many folk on their deathbeds, I have discussed the subject enough to know that few people complain in their waning minutes about wanting to spend a little more time in the office. It is more time with loved ones, more time doing the things that bring peace and joy that they grieve.

There is an old hymn that goes: "Now the day is over, night is drawing nigh..." I find myself humming it around the house lately. It's a healthy reminder of how quickly my life passes and how easy it is to waste precious time.

JUNE 21

I have absolutely no question that the resurrected Christ was a real and felt presence among the early church. There is no doubt in my mind that the people who were the first Christians were empowered by their conviction that Christ was alive and living among them. I believe the same is true today but how I describe that presence, how I explain that power may be significantly different than how it was explained two thousand years ago. And that's ok. Indeed, I believe it is vitally important that we find new ways of clarifying an experience that has been too often trapped in ancient explanations.

JUNE 22

For most of the two thousand years our religion has been in existence, we have been shaped by the story of humankind's inherent sinfulness. We were told that such a debased state of being makes us unworthy to be recipients of God's benevolence. We have sung of amazing grace, we have preached about unconditional love, but we haven't really believed it. We were taught that the breach between humans and God could only be bridged by a barbarous sacrifice. That the only way the wrath of God could be appeased was by the killing of God's own son. Now such an understanding may have made sense two thousand years ago when sacrifices were routinely made in the temple of Jerusalem but they hardly make any sense at all today. And yet we continue to talk and pray and sing as if they do. This is why I propose that we look closely at the teachings of Jesus rather than the teachings of Christianity. When we do we discover that Jesus' story doesn't always jibe with the stories we have been taught. We discover that Jesus' image of God is far more expansive than our own. We discover that grace is not something that needs to be earned by the faith that we have, the life that we live or even the death of Jesus. Grace is, Jesus tells us. It just is. It is all around us. It is in our midst. It is in every act of kindness, every gesture of forgiveness, every movement that brings people closer together. This is God. God is not some distant being sitting on a throne surrounded by yes men demanding this and commanding that. God is here. God is where two or three are gathered in love. God is where the Samaritan stops by the side of the road. God is when the father welcomes back his son. God is. That is the faith of Jesus rather than a faith about Jesus.

JUNE 23

I continue to believe that there is in creation a distinct reality that can cause two people to commit to each other for the rest of their lives as well as cause whole cultures to live in harmony and service. I believe this force has strength beyond my comprehension but I catch glimpses of it all the time. I see it at work in friends surrounding the bedside of a woman dying much too soon. I see it in the eyes of a mother holding her child or a volunteer building a house for someone who has none. The examples are infinite but they continue to serve as living proof to me that this force has a power greater than anything else in all creation. It cannot and has not been defeated by they vilest of wars, the hardness of cynics or the indifference of many. It continues to rise up from the ashes of hatred and violence, hunger and poverty, despair and death. It rises up over and over again and when I am awake, when I am ready, when I am open to its power, I rise up with it and my life has meaning again.

JUNE 24

For a Christian, the most dominant metaphor in scripture is death and resurrection. Our faith is predicated on the principle that out of death comes life. Although we certainly resist it, ours is a faith that remains true to the spirit of Jesus by always changing, always moving through the cycles of life, death and new life. Now, more than ever, we Christians must witness to the world of our willingness to go where Jesus went. "If any want to be my followers let them deny themselves and take up their cross and follow me." Our cross as Christians in America is to recognize and react to the enormous disparities that exist in the world. Our cross as Christians in America is to proclaim a God who blesses not one nation over another but all nations, all peoples.

JUNE 25

When people ask me why Jesus died I say because the Romans killed him. And the Romans killed Jesus because the religious leaders of the day convinced the Roman authorities that Jesus was a threat to their sovereignty. The religious leaders were good systematic theologians. They had a nice, neat plan all worked out for God. Indeed, they had spent centuries getting everything into place. It all made sense. Jesus, unfortunately for them, didn't make sense. He questioned their assumptions and rejected their suppositions. The religious leaders had very clever and very reasonable explanations for why the rich were rich and the powerful powerful. Jesus turned it all upside down. "Give it all away," he said to one surprised fellow. "Woe to you who are rich." he said to a whole congregation. "Blessed are the poor for yours is the kingdom of God." Such statements didn't make sense. Such declarations were dangerous! Thus, the logical thing to do was to destroy the declarer. And so they did.

JUNE 26

For Jesus, what mattered was not whether one was pure or impure. What mattered was that each and every person was a child of God. So Jesus doesn't go in for slaughtering pigeons or, and this is important for our consideration today, even baptizing people. Instead of engaging in ritual acts of purifying, Jesus throws parties. Instead of worrying whether sinners are right with God, Jesus invites them to sit down and eat. Imagine the scandal! Consider the confusion! Even John the Baptist doesn't know what to think so he sends two of his disciples to crash the party and ask, "Are you the Christ or should we look for another…because you're not behaving like any messiah we ever imagined!"

JUNE 27

It is a sappy sentimental film, I admit but lately that is really the only kind of movie I want to watch. I get enough realism in my daily life. It started around 2 in the morning and because I had nothing else better to do but worry, I sat down to watch. It was called "Sleepless in Seattle" and starred Tom Hanks and Meg Ryan. Although I admire Mr. Hanks and his great acting ability, I'd gladly give up a couple of hours of restless sleep for Meg Ryan.

Many of you know the story. Hanks is an architect whose wife has recently died. One night, at the instigation of his young son and out of his own loneliness, Hanks bares his feelings to a late night talk show host. When asked by the broadcaster how he will keep on going, Hanks carefully replied, "Well, I'll remind myself to take each breath and then I will remind myself to get out of bed and then I'll remind myself to put one foot in front of the other and then, maybe after a long time, I won't have to remind myself anymore."

JUNE 28

I am well versed in the doctrine of the resurrection. I have studied it from more angles than most Christians are even aware of. And I certainly understand that St. Paul made it very clear that if you don't believe in the resurrection the way he believed in it, you don't believe in it at all. But I think St. Paul is wrong. I think the resurrection comes in ways far more amazing than just flesh rising from the grave. Further, I think that you could find examples of just what I mean without me spending a whole lot more time telling you just what I mean.

JUNE 29

One of the best books I've read in recent years is Steven Levine's "One Year To Live".

It is a thoughtful work that has us pondering how we would spend the coming year if we knew it was our last. You cannot help but view springtime or your daughter's smile or an evening sunset differently when you know it may be the last time your ever get to enjoy them. The sadness of such thinking is tempered by the richness it brings to our experience. There is a proverb that says, "Live each day as if it were your last."

Easier said than done but utterly powerful when we do.

JUNE 30

Jesus' real enemies weren't the ones who wielded swords and marched in neat formations. Jesus' enemies came from within. Jesus' enemies were among those closest to him, his religious brothers. Jesus' real enemies were among those he worshiped with, those he ate with, those he walked with. Once again, I become overwhelmingly aware of the power of religious resistance. We all have wondered what would happen to Jesus if he lived out his life in our world and in our time. Most of us suspect the outcome would be pretty much the same.

JULY 1

One of the saddest and most accurate indictments of the church is that somewhere along the line we decided to decide for God just who deserves God's grace and who does not. It is absolutely amazing that Christians have actually wasted valuable time arguing over who is in and who is out, who is saved and who is not, who deserves and who does not. It is as if there is only so much of God to go around and so we had better be careful not to waste God on undeserving folk. I don't believe God grades on the curve. I don't believe there is only so much of God's love to share so only the folk in the top 10% get to go to heaven. I do believe that God isn't concerned with being fair but rather with being generous.

JULY 2

A student of mine asked: "Can I be confirmed if I don't believe in God?"

The Christian image of God can be enormously confusing to our kids because it runs the gamut from unconditional love to unbelievable hate. In my conversations with these students and others, I have found an increasing tendency to polarize beliefs. Often I will hear a young man or woman hesitatingly confess that they "believe in evolution" rather than God, as if it must be one or the other. In the current tenor of the times, this is understandable. Our children are bombarded with images of polarization, from every direction. Classmates, raised in a different Christian tradition than ours, can plant seeds of doubt with their own juvenile certainty. Quite early, our kids can begin to equate intellectual inquiry with faithlessness and because they certainly don't want to give up on learning, come to the conclusion that they don't believe in God.

Balderdash! I have said this before but it certainly bears repeating…the very reason Jesus called on us to become as little children was, I believe, because children have yet to lose their spirit of adventure, their joy at discovery, their love of imagination. The Kingdom of God is not something we carry around in our hip pockets or even locked away in our hearts. The Kingdom of God is the experience of the new. It is the encounter with resurrection. It is the realization that God is present in our lives but sometimes that presence comes in very surprising ways.

I'll stand with this student to announce that I sometimes don't believe in God either. I don't believe in a God who says I can't think. I don't believe in a God that demands unquestioning acceptance. I don't believe in a God that pits me against others or announces that some do not deserve. I don't believe in that God and I hope you don't either.

JULY 3

It is called the conspiracy of silence and it is well known in just about any academic seminary in America. Its definition is quite simple really. It is the admission that many pastors in mainline congregations aren't telling their congregations what they really know. Any clergyperson worth their salt has studied the Bible carefully and spent considerable time searching through the opinions and commentaries of hundreds of Biblical scholars but what many of us fail to do is relate the result of our research to our parishioners. Why?…because we have learned through painful experience that there are a lot of folk in the pews who don't want to hear it. There are a lot of folk who don't want to know the contradictions, inaccuracies, imperfections that are a part of their holy book. There are a lot of people who can make life very difficult for a pastor who points those intriguing scriptural curiosities out. So for decades, maybe even centuries, there has been this nasty little secret going on amongst the clergy: It's ok for us but not ok for you. A conspiracy of silence.

JULY 4

For two thousand years, Christians have been struggling with their relationship with the secular powers. All kinds of solutions have been proposed from religious dictatorships to experiments in religious socialism. St. Paul shaped much of our Christian understanding with a policy of appeasement. His sometimes desperate efforts to get along with the political authorities, even corrupt ones, have occasionally been used to bolster Christian cowardice in the face of governmental evil. In our own century the rise of the Third Reich was made increasingly easy with the attitude that Christians are bound to support their secular leaders.

We are, of course, bound only to Christ. When a government, a society, a teacher, a parent, a pastor go against the life and teachings of Christ, we are bound to resist them in the name of Christ. Conversely when these same people, institutions and others support the work of Christ, even if they are not Christian themselves, we are bound to support them. It was Luther himself who said he would much prefer a heathen Prince who ruled fairly than a Christian one who did not. So our guide then as we struggle with our Christian identity in America is Christ. If a policy rewards the rich and makes the poor suffer even more, how can we dare claim, as Christians, to support it? If violence is perpetuated, if selfishness is lauded, if the homeless are ignored and the poor are humiliated, how can we Christians affirm it?

JULY 5

When my sister-in-law died after a valiant battle with cancer, my wife and I flew back to Virginia to be with my brother and to help as we prepared for the funeral and the inevitable business that surrounds such sad times. One of our duties was simply to organize the many messages of condolence and the gifts of food that friends and particularly church members brought to the door. Now my brother isn't an overly pious type. He sings in the church choir although most summer Sundays you would find him sailing his ketch on the Chesapeake rather than sitting in a pew. But I will never forget what he said one day before the funeral as we drove along a lonely stretch of country road. We had been silent for a while and then he said, seemingly out of the blue, "I don't know how anyone could go through this without the church." Now I didn't question him on exactly what he meant by that but I suspect he wasn't talking about a particular doctrinal understanding, I don't think he was alluding to a specific creedal formulation or a precise Protestant principle. I believe he simply was referring to that spirit of compassion that marks a congregation of people who have discovered the healing power that comes in reaching out to others as Jesus did.

JULY 6

Late at night, I was watching Robin Williams' fine performance in "Dead Poet's Society". Anyone who has seen that classic film remembers the Latin phrase: "Carpe Diem". Seize the day. That is what Sabbath living calls us to do. Seize the day. This day. This moment. This life, here and now. Such wisdom, of course, is not limited to our religious tradition. Every religion, as far as I know, counsels the same. There is wisdom, divine, holy wisdom, in the invitation to Sabbath living whether it comes from the Holy Bible or the Tao-Ching. Lao-Tzu wrote: "Be content with what you have; rejoice in the way things are. When you realize there is nothing lacking, the whole world belongs to you."

JULY 7

Some of the sincerest people I know are religiously conservative Christians who have, I believe, a very distorted view of history and, far more importantly to our current concern, the future.

Some 50 million copies of author Tim LaHaye's apocalyptic "Left Behind" book series have been sold in this country in the last few years. One assumes it is a sincere attempt by both writer and readers to understand current events but, I humbly suggest, such sincerity could be catastrophic. No matter how sincere one is, the assumption that God destines the world toward a final cataclysmic battle certainly seems detrimental to any hope of peaceful negotiations with one's enemies.

Certain Christians are convinced that America has been chosen by God to be an instrument of divine purpose. One of those certain Christians is our president. His language in recent months reveals a growing conviction on his part that he is participating in God's plan of action. In January, in his State of the Union address he announced, "Liberty is not America's gift to the world. Liberty is God's gift to every human being in the world." Our military action planned for Iraq is, apparently, a divinely ordained destiny. "Events aren't moved by blind change and chance.", our president said at the Presidential Prayer Breakfast recently. "Behind all of life and all of history there's a dedication and a purpose, set by the hand of a just and faithful God." Sounds as if God has already chosen sides. Forgive me if I think such thinking may be a tad presumptuous.

JULY 8

One of the distinguishing marks of Jesus' parables is that they always subvert conventional wisdom. Nobody would think a heathen like a Samaritan would stop to help a Jew. No good Jew could imagine a father who has been so embarrassed by his son actually welcoming him back with open arms. No one could imagine God as a woman who lost a coin…God as a woman! Blasphemy! Except that Jesus said it. Jesus turned the tables on conventional wisdom just as he turned the tables upside down in the Temple.

JULY 9

"Teacher, what must I do to be saved?' asked the lawyer in the pin-striped suit. And Jesus told him this story: A man was going down from Denver to Colorado Springs and fell into the hands of robbers who stripped him, beat him and left him half dead. Now by chance a religious leader wearing a nicely ironed clerical collar was going down the same road and when he saw him he passed by on the other side. So likewise came a well-dressed politician with a flag in his lapel and when he came to the place and saw him, passed by on the other side as well. But a Muslim from Iraq while traveling came near him and when he saw him, he was moved with pity. He went to him and bandaged his wounds. Then he put him in his own jeep and brought him to a local hotel. The next day he took out money for two day's wages and gave it to the hotel owner and said, "Take care of him and when I come back I will repay you whatever more you spend." Which of these three, do you think, was a neighbor to the man who fell into the hands of the robbers?" The lawyer said, "The one who showed him a little kindness." And Jesus said to him, "Go and do likewise." And the crowd picked up stones and began muttering, "If you don't like our religion and you don't like our politics then why don't you just leave?" So Jesus did.

JULY 10

John was written after the other three gospels. In both Matthew and Luke, Jesus implores his disciples to love their enemies. No such talk in John. In John, Jesus tells his disciples not to love their enemies but each other. Could it be that by the time this book was written, around 100, the church had moved so far away from Jesus that they couldn't even get along with each other let alone with folk they considered their enemies?

JULY 11

Did you see the movie "About Schmidt"? It is an outstanding film starring Oscar winner Jack Nicholson and I just hated it. I hated it, I suppose, because it so accurately portrayed what Jesus proclaimed. I hated it because it announced what I so often do not want to hear…that a life without meaning is a life without serving. A life without meaning is a life lived ignoring the brokenness of the world, pretending it doesn't matter.

JULY 12

At the heart of Christianity, like it or not, is surprise. I suppose one of the greatest tragedies of our faith has been our incredible reluctance to be surprised. We want certainty. We want absolutes. And yet here we all are, identified with resurrection, identified with nothing less than the greatest of surprises. Go figure.

JULY 13

"You've changed" came the accusation. "Thank God" was my reply. Grace demands change. We simply cannot believe in the amazing grace of God and not have it alter our perceptions about everyone we meet. Grace surrounds that man whose politics are so different than mine. Grace surrounds that ill-dressed woman begging on the corner. Grace surrounds the bishop whose sexuality has become a national headline.

Grace surrounds you just as it surrounds me and that means our lives and our faiths are always going to be in flux. How dare we presume to take such a dynamic force as the love of God and try and codify and categorize it. All the creeds and confessions in the history of the church can't do it even while they pretend that they can.

JULY 14

Dietrich Bonhoeffer once said, "Jesus Christ exists as community." That is how he is made known. Not in doctrines of infallibility. Not in rituals of purity but in the community.

Recently I had the good fortune to undergo a couple of surgeries to relieve some significant pain in my neck. I know, I know, there are many saying I've been a big pain in the neck for so long it's only fair I feel what it's like…and, believe me, I have. The good fortune about the surgeries comes, of course, in the skill of the surgeon who has significantly eased my pain by fusing some vertebrae together but far more fortunate for me is the reawakening on my part to the importance of community. Nothing reveals the value of vulnerability than being vulnerable. How I cherished the cards and e-mails that surrounded me during those first two weeks of a long recovery! The prayers and phone calls, the gifts of food…oh, the breads…their symbol of life was powerful. There is a healing that happens when you know that others care about you. It is a healing far more tangible than sutures fading away or pain disappearing. It is a healing that inculcates hope. It is a healing that brings meaning. It is a healing that can only be described as a kind of salvation.

JULY 15

This week the Archbishop of Denver was featured on the front page of the NY Times declaring, as is his right, that there are some political issues for the Roman Catholic Church that are non-negotiable and anyone who claims to be in communion with the Catholic Church must abide by these non-negotiable principles. Again, I say that is certainly his right, perhaps even his duty, to state these doctrinal positions but I wonder how one can be so absolutely certain. Are there no extenuating circumstances?

I think of those folk who have gone through the anguish of deciding to have an abortion. I can remember vividly parents sitting in my office having to radically rethink their condemnation of homosexuality after learning that their own son had just come out of the closet. I think of Christopher Reeve who for nine years bravely sought radical new therapies for paralysis only to die of infection from a bedsore. All these and so many others that speak of exceptions to the rules. Do we damn them as evil? Do we relegate them to an ethical dung-heap? I can't. I suspect others can't either.

JULY 16

Much of Christianity today, particularly what has come to be known as evangelical Christianity, uses the lens of redemption in reading the Bible. This is summarized in the statement: "Jesus died for our sins." The earliest and most prolific writer of the Christian Scripture, Paul, uses this lens as well. For many Christians the Bible is viewed as a description of how God has acted in the death of Jesus to save a sinful world.

But not all Christians use this lens. Some of us have come to see the life and teachings of Jesus rather than the death of Jesus as a better lens by which to read the Bible. In so doing we swim against a traditional tide but we also discover a richness and meaning in the Bible that brings a richness and meaning into our own lives.

JULY 17

The Bible did not drop down from the sky, nor did God spend a few centuries dictating it to a privileged few. It is a work of literature that describes the thoughts, feelings, worldviews, philosophies of a variety of folk under a variety of conditions. The fact that it was brought together under one cover does not mean that one author wrote it. Think "Reader's Digest" rather than "Romeo and Juliet".

JULY 18

Now it won't come as any surprise to most of you that I think there are some saints who never set foot in church. Saints who by their actions and lives have imitated the Christ they never knew. Oh believe me I know there are many who parrot the phrase, "You don't have to go to church to be a Christian." but my hunch is that it is said more as excuse than cause for saintly action. I am thinking of those angels unaware who have dedicated their lives to sharing the gift of love outside of institutional boundaries. The temptation, of course, for those of us on the inside is to see these folks as less than saints but I think that can be less than a saintly action. There is an old Russian folk tale that speaks to this:

"Three monks lived on an island apart from any influence. They had no knowledge of religion and so they created their own: "We are three. You are three. Lord have mercy," they chanted all day every day of their simple life as they helped the island's other inhabitant with varied and sundry duties. One day a new bishop was appointed and he felt compelled to visit the monks although everyone else told him to forget them. When he arrived on the island he was astounded to discover that they three monks knew nothing of Christianity…not the creeds…not the commandments…nothing but their simple prayer: "We are three. You are three. Lord have mercy." Well, of course the bishop set about teaching them all that they had to know to be faithful followers of Christ. All day long he toiled and in the evening he left in his boat confident that he had done his duty and saved them from perdition. And so you can imagine the bishop's surprise when a half-mile out from shore the monks came to him walking on the water. They couldn't remember, they sadly confessed, what came after "Our father who art in heaven". "Go back to your simple prayer" the bishop said as he learned an important new lesson: Holiness comes through holy actions and never through just holy words."

JULY 19

Barbara Brown Taylor is a professor of preaching in a small school in Georgia but she is an inspiration to tens of thousands of preachers. She recently said, "In answer to people's faith questions, I hear myself saying things like; "What does it all mean? I haven't a clue. Do you?"

Such honesty can guide faithful Christians into the chaos knowing that glib answers and perfect plans are not in keeping with the spirit of Jesus, the one who risked the chaos of the compassionate life.

JULY 20

Not too long ago, I heard a confident young man declare: "The Bible says that God helps those who help themselves"...which God may very well do but it doesn't say so anywhere in the Bible.

Indeed, there is much that is publicly assumed about the Bible by people who probably don't know any better. Particularly dangerous is when these sure and certain spokespersons begin their declarations with: "The Bible clearly says..."

Such an introduction has been used with some frequency lately by folk who want to make sure we know just whose side God is on. The fact that God generally turns up cheering-on American, heterosexual Christians doesn't seem to phase their confidence. As the "Church Lady" is often quoted as saying, "How convenient!"

Another quote from a different church lady is this reminder from author Anne Lamott: "You can safely assume that you've created God in your own image when it turns out that God hates all the same people you do."

JULY 21

Here is an interesting exercise. Find a myth of a religion different than ours. Say it is the myth of Mohammad jumping on his stallion steed and galloping up to heaven or maybe even more bizarrely try a Hindu myth of a diety with a hundred arms or maybe the Greek god Zeus who after forcing his father to vomit up his brothers and sisters divides the universe into three parts. His brother Poseidon gets the water, his brother Hades gets the underworld and Zeus saves the heavens for himself. Does it all sound absurd to you? Does it bring a smile to your face as you shake your head in disbelief. But is it any more absurd than Moses parting the Red Sea or Noah riding out the flood with an ark load of animals or Jesus walking on the water and turning water into wine? Of course not. These are exercises in mythology not the scientific method. They are simply means for a more important message. The myths that shape our lives are no more factual than the myths that shaped or continue to shape the lives of millions of Hindus, Muslims or ancient Greeks. And yet because they are our myths many of us have decided they must be historical or they can't be true. Adam had to be the first, God had to stop the sun, Jesus had to walk on top of the lake. Such absurdities have Christians not only making ridiculous arguments with one another but stifling spiritual growth. To coin a phrase, we can't see the forest for the trees. We can't experience the wonder of God because we are trapped in the mundane minutia of our limited minds. When we literalize our myths we reduce our religion to nothing more than our own limited powers of reason. We put God in a box. We fool ourselves into thinking we can control God.

JULY 22

Traditional Christianity, the one most of us grew up with, is a faith more about Jesus than of Jesus. It is centered not on the life and teachings of Jesus but on his death and resurrection. The fundamental question for many in the early church was why Jesus died. After all, if he was who so many claimed him to be, how could God ever allow this terrible death by crucifixion? How could the messiah, the Son of God, be abandoned to such a horrible death?

Quickly, a theory developed that centered on the need to get back into the Garden of Eden. Because humankind's sinfulness was so great and so deplorable, the only way for reconciliation with God came in the sacrifice of a sinless being. Remember this is a world where animal sacrifices are commonplace and, indeed, even human sacrifices are not far removed from this time period. The idea captured the imagination of many and soon, very, very soon, even the teachings of Jesus were relegated to a secondary level of importance. What mattered was Jesus' death and the solution to religion's ancient problem. If Jesus would only die and take on the sins of the world, reconciliation would be accomplished. Guidelines were offered, faith was demanded, doctrines were written, creeds were developed…and the teachings of Jesus were relegated to the theological sidelines.

JULY 23

One of the reasons we Christians have been so reluctant to include Jesus in our lives is because he makes such a mess of them. When we seriously examine the way Jesus lived and the ultimate price he paid for living as he did, we get very nervous. We want Christianity to be about winning wars and coming out on top. We don't want to think about men hanging on crosses and giving up their lives. Truth to tell, Jesus may not be much help in the war effort. Wouldn't it be something if we actually turned to him in our efforts for peace?

JULY 24

One of the most profoundly moving passages in scripture for me comes in the fifteenth chapter of Luke: The three stories of the lost and found. Today we hear of the shepherd and the lost sheep, the woman and the lost coin. The other story is the famous tale of the prodigal son lost in a world of despair and self-destruction. What is so powerful for me are four words found in both these short parables. The shepherd looks for the sheep "until he finds it". The woman looks for the coin "until she finds it". Not until he gets tired. Not until he realizes he has 99 other bleating beasts to worry about. Not until it's time for dinner. Not until he just says to hell with it. None of that. The shepherd searches, the woman searches "until he finds it", "until she finds it". Such a metaphor evokes for me an image of God that is nothing short of amazing. This is a God who never gives up. In spite of the direst of odds, the tedious of tasks, God continues to search for those who have yet to know the wonder of love, the joy of living in forgiveness and grace.

JULY 25

I believe that too much of Christianity is under the control of the reasonable and the rational. I believe too much of Christianity is confined by the rules of what makes sense. We Christians have spent a good part of the last two thousand years trying to confine God to our limited reasons and explanations. We have written doctrine and developed dogma to satisfy our own desperate need to understand it all, to have it all make sense. We have even gone so far, so absurdly far, as to think that if people cannot accept our limited explanations of God then they cannot be accepted by God.

JULY 26

I believe that for two thousand years, Christianity has been captured not by the messiah revealed by Jesus' life and teaching but by the messiah that others wanted and expected. I suggest that this is why we have nothing about the life and teachings of Jesus in the very first records of Christianity, the writings of Paul. Perhaps Paul, just like John the Baptist, couldn't imagine a messiah who eats and drinks with sinners, who thinks it matters less what a man or woman believes and far more what a man or woman does. And even here we can see a decisive split between Jesus and early Christianity. From many accounts we have an image of Jesus who welcomes not just sinners, tax-collectors and the rest of that motley male crew but he welcomes women, as well. Women! Women, who were, in that society, nothing but chattel. Women, who were, according to Paul, not to speak up in church. What a scandal! How can he be the messiah? If we can't wait for another, let's remake him in our own image. And that is precisely what much of Christianity for the last two thousand years did and we have suffered because of it.

JULY 27

"Blessed are those whose sin is forgiven..." sings Psalm 32. There are times when human forgiveness may be impossible, when the situation is so dark and horrible that expectations of absolution are too remote to even consider. But beyond the pale of human ability and understanding there is God, a God, scripture tells us and Christ announced, who will not let anything stand between human and divine. It is to that God of unconditional love, of unremitting grace that we must turn at times, indeed in all times.

JULY 28

Violence may very well decide things but it doesn't solve things. In less than a hundred years we have fought the so-called WWI, the war to end all wars, the second world war in which millions of people died, the Korean conflict that solved nothing and the Vietnam War that solved even less. More recently there has been the Gulf War fought in between our watching the Irish Troubles, the Palestinian Conflict, the war in Serbia, the wars in Africa and on and on and on. And although decisions were certainly made, victors were joyously declared and losers punished and humiliated, none of it seems to have solved anything. Indeed, troubling as it may be, may I humbly suggest that the quiet death of one man two thousand years ago may have accomplished more in promoting good than all the so-called noble wars that have been fought in the intervening years.

JULY 29

Another maxim worth musing over is: "One today is worth two tomorrows." My friend Thich often reminds his students that we Americans are very good at preparing for life but not so adept at living it. We know how to sacrifice ten years for a diploma and we can work very hard to get a job or a house or a new car but we have great difficulty remembering that we are alive in the present moment, the only moment there is for us to be alive.

JULY 30

For most of our lives we have been told that being a Christian meant accepting Jesus as our personal Lord and Savior, or reciting this particular creed or accepting that specific doctrinal formulation. For millions and millions of folk, these understandings of God have served them well but I dare say there are others to whom these celestial concepts are difficult to grasp. For a variety of reasons, there are many good people who can, I believe, legitimately lay claim to being a Christian but who cannot experience the personal relationship or the doctrinal assumptions or the theological constructs. Good, decent, loving and compassionate, these folk are drawn to Jesus, drawn to the compassionate life, but unable to assimilate all of the language, all of the tradition, all of the rationale that has been shaped and molded over the last several millennia. Are such people damned to eternal destruction? I can't imagine it and that isn't just wishful thinking. My evidence is the life and teachings of Jesus.

JULY 31

There are many ways to faith. Some are simple, instant, firm. Others are more dependent on experience or logic and then there are those like some of me and maybe you, who stumble along the path, not exactly certain but not exactly not. We are the embodiment of the father's cry when Jesus heals his son, "I believe; help my unbelief!" Surely there are some who would claim that this wavering faith is not faith at all. Surely there are some who would demand complete allegiance or none at all. Surely there are those who would diminish the struggle some of us endure as we walk this way of faith and doubt, doubt and faith. Surely there are but just as surely there is me and maybe you who continue to claim to be Christian even when we're not too sure.

AUGUST 1

Why did Jesus die?

The simple answer is: The Romans sentenced him to death. He infuriated the worldly and religious powers and together they collaborated in his punishment. That's why he died. And just as the theories began flying after JFK's assassination, so did ones surrounding Jesus'. Over the centuries there were a myriad of different theories. They ranged the theological gamut but for a variety of reasons, the one that took hold within most of Christianity was the idea that he died to somehow atone for the sins of the world. It is time now to let go of this archaic and potentially very destructive understanding.

I do not believe Jesus died for the sins of the world. I believe Jesus died because of the sins of the world. That is, he spoke truth to power, he sought liberation for the powerless, he brought disruption to established order, and more, much more. Is it any wonder he was put to death?

AUGUST 2

It is pretty obvious to most of us that Jesus probably looked more like Yassir Arafat than Brad Pitt and yet Jesus continues to be portrayed in both secular and religious forums as if he just stepped off the bus from Iowa. Even the so-called historically accurate Mel Gibson movie "The Passion" had a Jesus of startlingly Anglo-Saxon qualities.

What gives?

The answer comes in what we get. We get a Jesus who not only looks like us and talks like us but thinks just like us. We get a Jesus who is so much like us that we figure he wouldn't do anything to upset us. We get a Jesus who blesses all that we do…including our bigotries and our bombings.

Curiously, in one of the last chapters of the gospel of Matthew, Jesus describes someone very different…"I was hungry and you gave me food, I was thirsty and you gave me drink, I was a stranger and you welcomed me, I was naked and you gave me clothing, I was sick and you took care of me, I was in prison and you visited me." So according to Jesus, Jesus doesn't look like Jesus, at least the Jesus people tell us he should look like. Instead he looks like the beggar on the streetcorner or the bum in the park. He's the one we make fun of for being different or weird or gay. He's the one on the outside looking in. Truth to tell, more often than not, he doesn't look much like us at all.

AUGUST 3

I believe to understand the Bible we must understand the context and time in which it was written. It is certainly not too difficult for most of us to understand how, two, three thousand years ago, folk like you and me could look out at their world and believe quite sincerely that the world was flat, the sky was round and the occasional volcanic eruption proved that hellfire and brimstone lay just below the surface. The ensuing years have proved otherwise. That doesn't make the ancients stupid or foolish but it does allow us the opportunity to understand the reasons why they wrote as they did. For us to <u>accept</u> their worldview however, given what we know now, would certainly make us appear most stupid and foolish. We know the world isn't flat. We know it took millions of years to develop and that it continues to change. We know that the heavens stretch far beyond the comprehension of most of us. We know all that. It is both stupid and foolish to pretend that we don't. And yet, so much of our religious language, concepts, hymns, even doctrine seem to do just that.

AUGUST 4

In the Gospel of Mark, Jesus is called the "Son of God" only four times. The first comes in the opening line: "The beginning of the gospel of Jesus Christ, the Son of God." Interestingly, the next three times Jesus is so described come out of the mouths of the most unseemly of folk. For instance, the second time Jesus gets called the Son of God it is from a host of unclean spirits who apparently know more than Jesus' own disciples. The next time comes when Jesus confronts the demon possessed fellow named Legion who has, according to Mark, something like two thousand evil spirits residing in his chained up body. The fourth and final time comes at the very end of the gospel and in a most surprising way. The centurion, the Roman soldier who had been in charge of crucifying Jesus, the very man who probably pounded the nails into Jesus' hands and feet, looks up to the cross and says, "Truly, this man was the Son of God!"

Now what I find so intriguing about these three incidents is the fact that they reveal the failure of the good guys, the religious guys, the disciple guys, to know who Jesus was. Everybody who ought to know doesn't, it seems. And those who shouldn't have a clue, do.

AUGUST 5

We were having dinner with some dear friends. Our host offered a beautiful prayer of gratitude before we sat down to a delicious meal. He was thankful not only for the food that was set before us and the friendship that we all shared but for a host of other gifts that we experience in our lives. The beauty of creation, the meaning that comes from serving others, the joy that love brings. And because one of the couples was leaving for Hawaii the next day, we also prayed for their safe travel. It was that last petition that brought me up short and set me to thinking more about this business of prayer and the role it plays in the lives of those of us who have entered into the New Reformation.

As our image of God moves from imaging an anthropological being up in the sky to something radically different, so too does our understanding of a myriad of other aspects and attitudes that shape what most people mean by calling themselves Christian.

If we no longer accept the notion, as I certainly no longer do, that God is a kind of glorified Santa Claus who curses those who are naughty and blesses those who are nice, then surely we must be asking ourselves about the efficacy of prayer. It certainly makes sense to me that we continue to express our concerns for the health and well-being of those we love and those we are called to love but what about praying for a safe trip? Does this mean that God could make it an unsafe trip? Does this mean that if God decided Hawaii wasn't the place God wanted our friends to be, God could pluck the plane right out of the sky and drop it into the ocean?

AUGUST 6

The rhythm of our world is out of whack when work becomes the reason for our being. When "What do you do?" becomes the indicator of who we are, you can bet we're in an unhealthy place. Sabbath brings us back into balance. "What do you do?"

"Well, I'm a lover. I'm a friend. I'm a carpenter. I'm a dad. I'm a wife. I'm a teacher. I'm a seeker." Sabbath reminds us who we really are.

AUGUST 7

President Bush has made no secret of the influence his evangelical Christian faith has had on his life. Clearly, some of it has been positive. But when that same faith shapes political and military decisions in a manner designed more to pacify God than the world, I worry.

When entire nations are characterized as "axis of evil" the implication is abundantly apparent: There are good nations and peoples and evil nations and peoples. And since God is always on the side of good nations then there is a divine imperative to eliminate the evil nations and peoples. This is not a political strategy. It is a religious one. This is the kind of religious strategy that has caused millions of innocent people to lose their lives. The Crusades, the Inquisition, the Holocaust, the annihilation of Hutus by Tutus and Tutus by Hutus are just some of the atrocities that come to mind when such religious language is evoked.

It is not unpatriotic for Americans to question such religious strategizing no matter how sincere it appears to be. Although we may be condemned to eternal perdition for doing so, we just may save the world in the process.

AUGUST 8

From the Zen tradition....

The disciple came to the master yearning for knowledge. The master carefully prepared tea. When it had brewed and the table was set, the master poured some tea from the pot into the disciple's cup. And when the tea reached the brim of the cup, the master continued to pour and the tea overflowed into the saucer and onto the table and then onto the floor and still the master poured. Finally the disciple cried out for the master to stop. The master said, "You are like this cup...so filled with your own opinions that there is no room for anything else."

AUGUST 9

Progressive Christianity is shaped primarily by the life and teachings of Jesus. That may seem self-evident but, in fact, many churches have consciously chosen not to make Jesus' life and teachings paramount. Instead, the primary focus is on the death and resurrection of Jesus. This begins with the writings of Paul, the earliest author in the New Testament. The gospels soon followed with similar sentiments and in a very short time Christianity lost much of its initial resource…the teachings of Jesus.

AUGUST 10

It's a funny thing about Peter. Here is a guy who makes more mistakes in his ministry than I did when I failed algebra and yet he is the one who comes out on the discipleship top. Peter is the one who not only denied he knew Jesus not once but three times, he consistently confused himself and others over what it meant to follow Jesus. Peter thought it meant success, triumph, a chicken in every pot. Peter promised he would follow Jesus to the death...as long as that death was only a nice metaphor for giving up a few things. Over and over again, Peter is depicted as anything but a brave and stalwart follower of Christ and yet, soon after Jesus is gone, there Peter is...right at the top.

I suspect the reason why Peter makes out so well has less to do with his leadership skills and more to do with the fact that he is a dead ringer for most of us. Who do you identify most with in the New Testament? Those with a messianic complex might say Jesus but I suspect the rest of us would fall firmly in the camp of Peter. Peter is everyman, everywoman. Peter promises and then doesn't deliver. He vows vigilance and then he immediately falls asleep. Peter is, in other words, you, me. Who better to be chosen to guide us in the way than someone who gets as lost as we do! You gotta love the guy!

AUGUST 11

I read somewhere that "hatred" in the Bible is best defined as a "simple lack of compassion". That should shake us to the core. Rather than excuse ourselves because we're not throwing rocks at tanks or turning fire hoses on protestors, we are forced to confront the reality that, at least for Jesus, hatred didn't involve emotional outbursts as much as no emotion at all. Hatred is simply not caring. The opposite of love isn't hatred. It is indifference.

AUGUST 12

"A little yeast leavens the whole batch of dough" is how the Apostle Paul puts it in Galatians. It's a proverb worth pondering whenever we have to wait for the yeast to rise. We can use our yeast time musing over the little seeds of faith that are planted by so many of us without either knowing what we're doing or seeing immediate results. I have long been convinced that the brash and brazen demand for immediate religious change is both slightly foolish and ultimately futile. "Repent!" screams the sidewalk preacher or the perfectly coiffed man on TV and the folks gather and the aisles are filled with weeping sinners while the organ plays "Just As I Am". There is, to be sure, a sense of poignancy and pathos in all of that but I do wonder about its efficacy. Luther said that every born-again Christian should go into a closet for six months to ponder what has happened. Having been the victim of accosting new believers, I concur with Dr. Martin's advice. Like yeast the Holy Spirit needs time to rise, to do its holy work. Rush it and the bread falls flat.

AUGUST 13

All you really need to know about Christianity can be found in Luke 15. There are three stories. A lost sheep whose shepherd refused to stop looking until he found it. A lost coin whose owner refused to stop looking until she found it. And a lost son whose acceptance back home was based not on his confession of sins, not on his admission of guilt, not on his willingness now to follow all the rules, his acceptance was based on grace, amazing, unmitigated, unending grace. Enter deeply into the reality of those three stories and I promise you that your life will change…as will your faith.

AUGUST 14

I don't think you can be a Christian in isolation. The very claim that we follow Jesus demands, it seems to me, a relationship with others. One cannot be a disciple and not seek to bear the suffering of others. This is one of the great values of the institutional church: it gives us the opportunity to bear the sufferings of others. Even when we want to hide from the pain and agony that fills so much of the world, our institution calls out and reminds us of our obligations. Even when we want to avoid thinking about the genocide in the Sudan, the starvation in East Africa, the hatred being cultivated against those different than us...the church refuses to be silent. Salvation comes not by acquiescing to doctrines about love but by loving others as Christ loved others, by forgiving others as Christ forgave, by welcoming as Christ welcomed.

AUGUST 15

One of the most intriguing verses in all of the passion story comes as Jesus speaks to his disciples around the Passover table. Jesus announces that one of these friends will betray him. And what do the disciples do? "And they began to question one another which of them would do this." Don't they already know? Don't they have a sense of right and wrong? Don't they have the moral gumption to proclaim for all the world to hear that they are absolutely positive what they are going to do and what we should do as well?!!!

Of course not. Of course not because the wisdom of Luke and Matthew and Mark reveals that anyone, even those closest to Jesus, is capable of the ugliest of actions. "Is it I?" the disciples ask Jesus in Mark's account. Surely they should know...but they don't. They don't because they are being utterly honest. They don't because they know that anyone given particular circumstances can do the vilest of deeds. "Is it I?" should be the question all of us are asking of ourselves when we so quickly condemn others as being wrong, stupid or evil.

AUGUST 16

It is much easier to simply accept what others have accepted and forego our own questions and conclusions. But following Jesus is a risky business. It does demand an openness and vulnerability that many find too high a price to pay. It does demand that compassion take precedence over everything else...even our own religious traditions. Is that a paradox? Yes. It is also the way of Christ.

AUGUST 17

I'm of the ilk that has me cringing when some dear friend declares that they are going to read the Bible from cover to cover. It is a noble task and I certainly wouldn't want to discourage it but my bet is that most folk are going to get bogged down by Leviticus and give up long before they ever get to Revelations. That's because the Bible isn't meant to be read like a novel. I think it can be far more helpful to focus on particular passages that may be of much greater relevance to you than others. Personally, I'm not all that interested in the dietary laws of ancient Israel. If they don't want to eat a sea gull or a scallop that's certainly OK by me, I just don't see where it matters much to my own journey of faith.

I turn to the tales of Jesus for most of my spiritual edification. I especially like the parables, and especially the parables found in Luke, they may be the most authentic pieces in the New Testament. I also think they are the very best way to begin reading the Bible for children. The story of the Good Samaritan or the Prodigal Son evokes rich images for kids as well as adults.

AUGUST 18

One of the most frustrating aspects of the ministry of Jesus is how little we really know of it. We have really so little hard evidence of what he thought or taught or did. A few pages…from maybe a year of his life, no more than two. That's it. And out of these few shreds of evidence we have constructed a vast system of beliefs that have shaped and formed most of western civilization. And exactly how much of it is based on the actual teachings of Jesus? Not much. Very little, really. Because the truth of the matter is civilization probably would have crumbled long ago if we actually did what Jesus would do.

AUGUST 19

Yes, Jesus was a Jew and yes, so were Matthew and Paul and Mark and John and others but must their family squabbles continue to shape our 21ˢᵗ century theology? Isn't it time we put all vestiges of our anti-Jewish bias behind us? Why can't we turn to Judaism and say "Thanks for the start but we're going to take it from here. Good luck and Godspeed to you and to us as well 'cuz I suspect we're all headed in the same direction anyway."

AUGUST 20

A drive through most cities, a visit to almost any urban public school, will quickly provide evidence that America continues to belie our public conviction that "all men are created equal". Most of us privately admit that some are more equal than others.

Compassion literally means, "to share hearts". Sharing hearts may mean we have to step down from time to time in order that others might step up. Such sacrifice may not appear fair in the short term but surely a few centuries of past unfairness make our complaining seem petty.

AUGUST 21

I believe the only healthy religions are those religions that balance the masculine and the feminine, that recognize the importance of uniting the male and female into a cohesive and beautiful whole. The religious world that Jesus entered was a world that had forgotten this truth. What Jesus did was bring the feminine gifts of compassion, forgiveness and acceptance into that world. He saw the need for balance. He saw the need for that cohesive, beautiful whole. He saw it but few others did and so he was killed; killed, one might hypothesize, by a world that refused to be shaped by a myth of motherhood.

Such a hypothesis may not be as far-fetched as we might first assume. Mary Daly once wrote, "When God is male, all males are gods." Such reasoning certainly seemed to pervade the world of Jesus where women were bought and sold like cattle. There was a prayer offered in the synagogues in Jesus' time that began, "Blessed art Thou, O Lord, who hast not made me a woman." Into that world came one whose very life flew in the face of such sentiment. Jesus offered a radical new perspective on the kingdom of heaven and the image of God. It was not limited to one kind, one way, one gender. It incorporated the myth of motherhood, the gifts of femininity. Of course, Jesus saw God as father. He, too, was a product of his time and culture but in one of the only examples in the gospels of Jesus' actual language, the language of Aramaic, Jesus addresses God as "Abba". And the best definition we have of "Abba" is "Daddy", the gentlest, most feminine form of father.

AUGUST 22

There has been a terrible arrogance in Christian thought for far too long. We have twisted scripture to convince ourselves that anyone who doesn't agree with our theological perspective is not only wrong but deserving of eternal damnation. The horrors of history have often been perpetrated on this very point. Living here in the West, one needn't look far to see what the so-called Christian mindset allowed in the settling of these territories. Indigenous people, folk who celebrated their spirituality in ways different than Christianity, were deemed not only pagan and heathen but less than human. Because of Christian arrogance, these people were deemed inferior. And because Christianity didn't honor the biblical tradition of respecting other truth seekers, we found it easy to brush their wisdom aside. Indeed, we found it quite easy to simply eliminate tribes and tribes of wise men and women.

AUGUST 23

The uniqueness of Christianity is found, of course, in our belief that in Jesus of Nazareth the mystery of God was embodied. In this gentle man's life and teachings, in his death and the wonder of his resurrection, we touch the eternal, we realize the divine. And it is "unto us" that this happens. It is not reserved for only the pious or the priest. It is not limited to only the religious or the righteous. This man, this God, is for us, all of us. You, me, them. Believer, doubter, agnostic and atheist. God comes for us. For all of us. And despite the attempts of countless claimants, no one person, no one institution, no one religion can limit this God who comes for all, for us.

AUGUST 24

Purgatory is a mythological concept that allows us not only to describe the end-
less grace of God but also the importance of recognizing our need for it. In that
tale from Luke 15, the prodigal son wallows in the pigsty until, the Bible tells us,
"he came to himself". Purgatory can be a place where we too can come to ourselves, where we can realize the depth and richness of God's love for each and
every one of God's creation. Certainly there are vast numbers of Christians who
say we have to reach such a realization in this life or we are lost forever. But I
would suggest that the concept of purgatory is more in keeping with the teachings of Jesus than this other, more limited and, quite frankly, terribly unloving,
un-Christ-like image of God.

AUGUST 25

I don't apologize for my conviction that fundamentalism is the greatest enemy of authentic Christianity. Fundamentalism is reason run amuck. It is the absurd assertion that God can be reduced to a set of rules. No matter how pious those fundamentals may appear, they are, by their very nature, antithetical to the God revealed by Christ. For this is a God who refuses to be bound by rules no matter how holy we might claim they are. When I hear the arguments some Christians make for disallowing women in ministry or refusing gays for membership or condemning others to hell, I am reinforced in my conviction that the God they worship is not the God revealed by Jesus. It is, rather, a God shaped by dishonest theologians desperate to have everything make sense.

AUGUST 26

It is called the "slippery slope" argument and it is used by too many theologians and pastors, Bible-study leaders and seminary teachers. Essentially it argues that if we allow one of our ancient presuppositions to be questioned, what will stop the questioning of all presuppositions? It is played out, for instance, when biblical literalists demand that every word of the Bible is historically accurate in spite of its obvious errors and contradictions. It is played out when a hierarchical church demands obedience to its leaders even when those leaders are found to be morally suspect or worse. Any breach in the armor, any crack in the wall, they are afraid, will bring the whole thing tumbling down. And so Christians have been told for two thousand years that you can only question so far, you can only think so much. Don't push it. Don't challenge it. Don't. Don't. Don't.

But some of us do. Some of us are finding that in our own reading and our communal conversations, new and exciting discoveries are being made. Our spiritual lives are being reactivated, our faith is being reborn. These are exciting times but they are also disruptive times. These are times when assumptions are being questioned and hypotheses reexamined.

AUGUST 27

A quote from the inimitable Oscar Wilde, author, bon vivant, society's critic and also its outcast and once, believe it or not, a guest star at the opera house in Leadville, Colorado…"We are all living in the gutter but some of us are looking at the stars."

A discomforting image perhaps but not without some merit and certainly worth our pondering.

Almost every night when the darkness has descended, my wife and I turn off all the lights in our house and tip toe to our leaky old hot tub that sits out under the open sky. It is not just our time for reacquainting our lives but putting them into perspective as well. Lying out under the sky and looking up at the stars instills in us always a sense of wonder and often a whisper of hope.

AUGUST 28

I do not understand Jesus in doctrinal terms. I do not see him as an instrument of atonement who, in some bizarre way, demands our intellectual loyalty as a ticket to eternity. Rather I see Jesus as the epitome of compassion. The more I read and study his life and teachings the more I am convinced of this truth. For me to claim to be a disciple of Jesus, I must seek to enter into the world of compassion that His life and death and resurrection point me toward.

AUGUST 29

Have I ever told you about the half-smile? It's a wonderful way to be fully in the present. Sit up straight. Feet on the floor. Breathing deeply…now form your mouth into a half-smile. Not a full stretch or a tiny grin, but half way in between. Do you feel yourself relaxing? It's amazing isn't it? And you can take that half-smile everywhere you go! Looking off onto the mountains, give them a half-smile and feel yourself grow closer. Watching a child at the supermarket, half-smile and see if you don't immediately feel a bond grow between you. Half-smile at the preacher during a sermon and tell me if you don't understand the sermon better when you do.

AUGUST 30

Some friends bring a paralytic to Jesus to be healed. Jesus' home is so crowded that they literally tear down the roof to get their friend close to Jesus, close to God. And what does Jesus say? Does he ask the paralyzed man if he has a personal relationship with God? Does he demand that the man recite a confession of faith or memorize the Ten Commandments? No. The Bible says that when Jesus saw the faith of the man's friends, he healed him. What a curious thing! This man's healing, this man's forgiveness, this man's salvation is determined not by his own faith but the faith of those who love him. Here's a new one for St. Peter at the pearly gates: "Have you accepted Jesus as your personal Lord and Savior?' "No, but my friend has." "Well, that's good enough for me. Come on in!" Suddenly in these few words from Mark, we have an expanding, expansive image of the kingdom. Suddenly in five words, we are confronted with an image of grace that goes far beyond the limited, private perception that has been promoted to the exclusion of all others.

AUGUST 31

I believe that we have been operating for far too long with a misunderstanding of what it means to believe. Somewhere along the line, Christianity moved from being a way of life to a system of beliefs. Soon after Jesus' death, we got real nervous over the idea of just following him and began to write down what it really meant to be a Christian. Soon those written words became more important than the simple following. Soon people could call themselves Christian without ever knowing anything about Jesus.

Look at the Apostle's Creed. "I believe in Jesus Christ, his only Son, our Lord. He was conceived by the power of the Holy Spirit and born of the virgin Mary. He suffered under Pontius Pilate was crucified, died and was buried." What happened to everything in between? What happened to his life of reaching out to the oppressed, feeding the hungry, forgiving the sinner? Suddenly being a Christian meant accepting beliefs about Jesus instead of actually following Jesus. That isn't faith. Faith isn't about believing. Faith is about trusting.

SEPTEMBER 1

What are we to make of Jesus' death? If it wasn't to take on the sins of the world and somehow appease a petty and angry God, is there any meaning at all that we can get from this tragedy?

We can see the death of Jesus as a revelation of the nature of God. Jesus certainly had options. He didn't have to die the way he did. He could have chosen to fight. He could have organized the Zealots, who were abundant in his time, into an army of guerilla fighters and taken on Rome. He could have debated his cause in court. Clearly he was a gifted orator; perhaps he could have moved the masses onto his cause and turned the judicial tables upside down. He could have run away. He could have done all manner of things than what he did. But in submitting to the injustice, in silently bearing the beating and humiliation and ultimately hanging from a cross like a common criminal, he revealed a God whose love is so deep, so profound, so powerful, that nothing can compare to it. Might it have been the purpose of Jesus in his death to show that violence, hatred, anger when met by love become powerless? Yes, he died but in his death the hypocrisy of the powers was revealed, the emptiness of religious authority exposed and a movement was born that continues to this very day, a movement that reveals the nature of God in every act of peace and justice, in every gesture of kindness and mercy, in every act of sacrificial love.

SEPTEMBER 2

And Jesus increased in wisdom and in stature…"

Not only did Jesus physically grow up but, according to Luke, he intellectually matured as well. This is rather remarkable when you think on it. I suspect that most folk who call themselves Christians might take exception to Luke's statement. Most Christians, of course, have never really read the Bible and so it is not surprising that this verse could be considered scandalous. After all it implies that Jesus was not all-knowing from the very beginning. It implies that Jesus was not the perfect divine creature but rather a normal human being who slowly grew into the awareness of the realities that surrounded him and the spiritual path he felt called to follow. It really is a remarkable concept to contemplate. Jesus changes. Jesus moves from a wide-eyed boy to a curious teen to a mature man. He grows in wisdom and in stature. He develops his world-view. He shapes his existential understanding. He changes his mind.

SEPTEMBER 3

In the time of Jesus, miracle workers were plentiful. Virgin births were relatively commonplace. Even raisings from the dead were reported with a certain regularity. That was the world of Jesus and the world of those who eventually wrote about him. We need to understand that so we can better understand Jesus. With very little effort, I could offer you birth stories about other gods that circulated around the time of the writing of the New Testament that include guiding stars, angel visitation, shepherds' instructions, and, of course, virgin births. This was simply a means of honoring those they believed deserved honoring. The stories that surround the birth of these gods, including Jesus, were not attempts at deception but rather tribute. I accept them as such. I do not accept them as fact. I no more believe as fact that Jesus was born of a virgin than I believe the world is flat or the heavens stop a few thousand feet above my head.

SEPTEMBER 4

I find it more than a little discouraging at times to witness the many ways folk have claimed Jesus' benediction on their own way of thinking. They may be doing all kinds of good and beneficial things but I have to say they're pretty loose with their understanding of what it means to call Jesus the Son of God. For instance, there is a certain organization in Colorado Springs that urges us to focus more closely on our families. A good thing, I dare say, to do. They raise millions of dollars and influence tens of millions of people, I suppose. They claim this is what it means to follow Jesus. But you would be very hard pressed to find anything in the teachings of Jesus that would have us focusing on the family. Indeed, Jesus seems to say just the opposite. His image of the family is much broader than just biology. Or we might look at the way Christianity has been usurped by certain politicians to imply that being a loyal American is a very Christian thing to do. I certainly believe in being a good American but once again I think you would find it very difficult to locate anything in the teachings of Jesus to support patriotism. Jesus' idea of community wasn't limited to one way of thinking, one way of acting, even one way of believing. Or, we have all heard, in one way or another, the implication that wealth is a blessing from God. The more we have the more God has blessed us. And, once again, as much as I love having things, I don't think you have a snowball's chance in hell of finding anything in the teachings of Jesus to support what is clearly an illegitimate claim.

September 5

When we don't get what we want, some people assume it is because God has something better or at least different in mind. This may make some sense until what we wanted was our child to recover from leukemia or our spouse to make it through chemo. When they don't it can be exceedingly difficult to accept that God had something better in mind for them. Such an understanding runs the risk of doing a couple of destructive things. The first is creating an enormous animosity toward God. If God could have helped and didn't, who wants to have anything to do with God? The other may be even more diabolical. It centers on the idea that we didn't do enough to urge God into action. If only we would have prayed more or said certain words or had more faith…it's our fault that our child died, our spouse didn't make it.

Both are terribly destructive. Both continue to be, sometimes subtly, sometimes not, perpetuated by the church.

SEPTEMBER 6

"Remember the Sabbath and keep it holy." This is not an order but an invitation, an invitation into a richer, fuller, more meaningful life. Some people believe that there are certain places in this world where the separation between this life and the next is very thin. It may be a mountaintop in the Rockies or a cathedral in Europe. These are the sacred spaces that we treasure and cherish. But I believe this thinness can be found not just in a place but in a time and that time is here and now, each time, every time we remember the Sabbath and keep it holy.

SEPTEMBER 7

What are we so afraid of in the church? Because that is precisely why we seek to keep the gospel away from others. We demand they do this or think that before they can possibly approach our all-loving God. Why have we forgotten that even the most refined doctrine, even the most beautiful of rituals are only meager guides, brief glimpses of the amazing grace of God. Whenever the institution begins to believe that they are the only means of God's grace, look out because here comes Jesus weaving together a cleansing whip.

SEPTEMBER 8

I don't know where I heard this story but it certainly bears repeating…

A man went on a search for the kingdom of heaven. He often complained how miserable the world was becoming and how the community was going downhill fast. One day he set out on a journey to find a better place. He walked all day until it was growing dark. Then he smoothed down the ground and prepared to sleep for the night. Before he lay down, he put his shoes in the middle of the trail and pointed them in the direction he had been heading. During the night, a man came by and couldn't resist the practical joke so he turned the shoes back toward where the man had come. In the morning the man got up and walked in that direction. He walked all day until it was growing dark. Then he came upon a city. It was vaguely familiar. He entered a street that looked very much like his own. He knocked on a familiar door and greeted the family he found there. "This must be heaven," he said.

SEPTEMBER 9

The most popular understanding of Jesus death is that he somehow took on the sinfulness of humankind and atoned for such evil by suffering a terribly painful and humiliating death. Such an understanding runs the risk of objectifying Jesus, making him into nothing more than an object of sacrifice, a scapegoat or to put it in familiar liturgical language…"the lamb of God who takes away the sins of the world." Progressive Christians honor Jesus' death not as some kind of proscribed and horrific ritual to appease an angry God but as a powerful, life-changing symbol of how far a loving God is willing to go to manifest grace. What does it really mean to love the world? Jesus shows us in his willingness to die as a witness of the power of love rather than recant to save himself. Jesus' life and teachings are the primary force in our understanding of what it means to be Christian.

Now if you are paying attention you are probably quietly asking yourself if such an understanding is heresy. And the answer is yes. But heresy is always getting a bad rap. Heresy is simply another view outside the norm. Martin Luther was a heretic. Indeed up until very recently the Vatican deemed all Lutherans heretics. Heresy has a noble tradition, an honorable past and, I dare say, a very important role in the future.

SEPTEMBER 10

My understanding of what happened in Jerusalem on that first Pentecost: The spirit of God became accessible to those folk gathered together and suddenly they began to understand the truth in their own language, in their own way. And this is not just a miracle of linguistics. The different languages that were spoken on that day are surely a metaphor for something much bigger than a room filled with Spanish and French and Greek and West African speakers. This is a moment of transformation when suddenly the gospel message, the good news of God's immeasurable love begins to make sense and it makes sense because people hear it in their own way, their own time, their own rhythm, their own custom, their own images, their own language.

SEPTEMBER 11

I am convinced that Jesus manifested a life of compassion. Compassion means literally "the sharing of hearts". He identified with others and not just those who looked like him or believed as he did. He shared hearts with the rejected prostitute at the well, the despised tax collector at the gate, the ridiculed rich-man in the tree. To share hearts is to seek common ground, mutual understanding. When we enter into relationships convinced that our way is the only way we prevent the true sharing of hearts, we deny compassion. One of the great joys of getting older is the stunning recognition that all that you were so convinced of earlier in your life isn't all that convincing later in your life. The wisdom that can come from aging is an openness to the wisdom of others. Traveling can do this as well, traveling outside the prescribed tourist routes and into the lives of folk who seem, at least at first glance, very different than you. But as you share hearts, as you enter into each other's wisdom, you discover a commonality that transcends politics or theology and binds you to another child of God. Surely this is what Jesus knew and did over and over again.

SEPTEMBER 12

Often the most effective means of sharing our faith comes in very quiet, humble ways. As we go about our lives of faith, displaying our allegiance to this God of love by the way we live out our lives, the decisions we make, the forgiveness we share, the love and sacrifices we offer, the yeast, so to speak, begins to bubble. God is at work in very humble, ordinary ways. Sometimes, many times, it all takes time. Conversion should be a slow process. The yeast rises on its own, we cannot rush it. All we can do is set the process in motion and let the spirit do her work.

SEPTEMBER 13

I certainly will admit that rapture theology is dramatic and captures the imagination but it is also terribly divisive and inherently violent, two characteristics that must never be associated with Jesus. Rapture theology pits us against them. It says some are saved and some are not and of course those who are saved are the ones who agree with us. On my e-mail signature I have a quote from Anne Lamott, "You can safely assume you've created God in your own image when it turns out God hates all the same people you do."

SEPTEMBER 14

Most of Christian history is filled with acts of arrogance. Arguments have been offered, battles waged, over similar foolishness. We've heard people claim everything from apostolic succession to the need to be born again. We've watched as so-called Christians have demanded one-way thinking and damned anyone who disagreed. We've even witnessed the abomination of some Christian churches denying the sacrament to those seeking to meet Christ. I wonder if there can be any sadder question than the one I get occasionally from visitors here when they ask if they can receive communion even though they are strangers. We've pretty much seen it all, haven't we? And yet we seem to learn as slowly as the original twelve, which means hardly at all.

SEPTEMBER 15

In my study of the life and teachings of Christ, I've come to be convinced that nothing matters more to Jesus than compassion. All the doctrine the church has compiled, all the dogma that fills our shelves, all the bishops that have been crowned and pastors ordained…all of it matters not a whit if it is not centered in compassion. To be compassionate is to literally share one's heart. It is to so identify with others that their joy becomes your joy, their sadness your sadness, their pain your pain.

Anytime the church forgets that at our heart is compassion, the church fails to follow Jesus. Even when we couch it in the churchiest of language, if it isn't fundamentally and deeply compassionate, it is not the teachings of Jesus. Whenever we in the church use ancient doctrines or treasured theologies to keep outsiders outside, we fail Jesus. When Christians claim that their refusal to allow certain folk entrée into the church is based on the Bible, they may have honored a book but they have failed Jesus. When Christian leaders demand unquestioning allegiance to policies and positions that are not compassionate in intent, they have left Jesus behind no matter how holy it all may appear.

SEPTEMBER 16

"Ecclesia semper reformanda est."

It means the church is always in need of reform. And that motto, as fundamental as it is to the Protestant tradition, is often ignored, even vilified, by those who too often confuse Christianity with the comfortable life.

SEPTEMBER 17

The Bible is a copy of a copy of a copy…and maybe a few copies more. Actually we have to begin with no copies because much of the Bible is based on an oral tradition that preceded any writing down of events or stories. Oral traditions are notorious, of course, for slightly changing each time they are told. Witness the old game of "Party Line" where you sit in a circle and someone whispers a simple sentence to the person next to them and tells them to pass it on. By the time it makes its way around the circle it is often unrecognizable from its origin! Remember that just in the New Testament alone we have a decidedly lengthy time between the life of Jesus before the gospels are written…as much as seventy years. A "Party Line" that lasts that long is bound to have some real changes made to the original stories.

A bigger question, of course, is: Does this oral tradition make our written stories less valid? No, not at all but it does make them less a resource for historical accuracy and more an explanation of what mattered to the storytellers as time goes by. This is why Matthew, Mark, Luke and John have some significant differences in their tales of Jesus. One is not more right than another, just different.

September 18

I've seen the books that fill the shelves that promise following Jesus will bring financial success or personal rewards. I've seen the covers that announce: "Jesus as C.E.O." or Jesus as "The Greatest Salesman That Ever Lived." Clever titles and sometimes even clever theses all wrapped in the warm and fuzzy teaching of warm and fuzzy Jesus. Only problem is they aren't...the teachings of Jesus, I mean. They can be good and clever exercises in self-improvement, they can help us build successful businesses or even happy homes, all of which is wonderful and good, but most often they don't have much to do with the teachings of Jesus.

SEPTEMBER 19

One of the dramatic changes in progressive Christianity is the recognition that this creation of God's is good. Not perfect to be sure but not utterly depraved either. Despite the ancient stories and despite the modern evangelicals, many of us Christians simply reject the idea that we are, to use the words of my Lutheran childhood, "by nature sinful and unclean". "God don't make junk" is the way one bumper sticker put it and I concur. For far too long we have elevated the teachings of Paul and his obsession with our need for redemption at the expense of the inclusive teachings of Jesus.

SEPTEMBER 20

"One can always be kind to people about whom one cares nothing," Oscar Wilde.

I think of that quote often when I am tempted to romanticize my concern for those less fortunate. It is so very easy to talk glibly of the plight of the poor, the oppressed, the homeless. It is quite another thing to get to know them.

You may find it as easy as I do to quickly write off a check to our favorite charity, content in the satisfaction that we have fulfilled our altruistic obligation.

The truth, of course, is that such activity often simply shields us from having to really get involved with those people we would just as soon forget.

Because of where I work, I often have the opportunity to meet a wide variety of folk who are down on their luck. On far too many occasions, I find myself not wanting to hear their tales of woe. It's not that I won't help them. I usually do. But my help comes from a checkbook or a wallet and not from the heart. I don't want to have my life interrupted by having to get to know these unfortunate visitors.

I sometimes wonder how many fascinating people and interesting stories I have missed out on by my reluctance to listen, my hesitation to really care. Mr. Wilde's prophetic word is a constant critique and a valued reminder.

SEPTEMBER 21

It is very interesting to note that the early church, shaped on the teachings of Jesus, was very open to women, even to women in leadership roles. But very quickly, within the first fifty years of development, the old ways began to assert themselves and women were, once again and in direct defiance to the teachings of Jesus, reduced to second-class status. It is the late book of Timothy, probably written toward the end of the first century that has that foolishness about not permitting women to teach because Eve was the one who, according to that author, brought sin into the world. Gee, I wonder if a man wrote that?

SEPTEMBER 22

I find it a curious paradox that although Christianity leads us to Jesus, it often hides the spirit of Christ from us. Too many examples exist of how a narrow perspective of God working in this world prevents us from experiencing the presence of Christ all around us. I honestly believe that if we limit God to our own time or tradition, we have failed to grasp the wonder of the Christ experience. The spirit of God cannot be contained by one moment in history, one place in geography, one rather narrow theological perspective. What I often see among us Christians is great knowledge and little wisdom. The demand for rigidity of belief leaves little room for revelation. When we think we know it all we close the door on God, the God who lives today and not just 2000 years ago. To proclaim the resurrection of Christ is to stake our faith in a God who can never be contained; not by history, not by a tomb, not even by a particular religious perspective.

SEPTEMBER 23

Within the holy catholic church, we have a number of denominations that refuse to allow particular people to share in Holy Communion. It is the Christian tradition, of course, that Jesus instituted this sacrament and asked, some might say commanded, us to "Do this in remembrance of me." The denial of access to this holy event is invariably based on doctrine. It depends on whether an outsider believes as those on the inside believe. It is quite clear to me an abomination and an insult to the memory of Jesus. But it is precisely what happens when we forget that Christianity was intended to be a way of life and not another religion. When creeds come before compassion we have dishonored Jesus and disregarded his central teaching: "Be compassionate as your father is compassionate."

SEPTEMBER 24

Two people go to a concert. One is a musician to her fingertips. She has spent her life studying, practicing, enjoying the fruits of the musical world. He is bored to tears. He can't wait until intermission. He has never been captured by the beauty, the richness, the wonder of the musical world. They sit together but there is a great divide between them. And no matter how hard she may try, she cannot force the man to share in her pleasure. Her hope is only that sometime, somewhere he will begin to see what she has known all along.

Is it not possible to conceive in our imaginations a time and place where such seeing can take place? Is it not possible to imagine that our death is not necessarily the end of our spiritual journey but a continuation of the same? The concert was heaven for her but hell for him. Should he be condemned for his lack of understanding? Or should we keep playing beautiful music "until he finds it"?

SEPTEMBER 25

I'm convinced that one of the greatest impediments to a more mature and evolving faith is rooted in our hymnody. Of course, much of our music is written with metaphor but too many of us have failed to understand it. We have used our hymns to continue to repress spiritual growth. In nearly every other walk of life, our art, music, poetry and more have incorporated the context of time and place to proclaim the message. Unfortunately, too much of Christian art has failed to do the same. That is why we get hymns like this one;

> "Onward Christian soldiers, marching as to war
> with the cross of Jesus going on before.
> Like a mighty army moves the cross of God.
> Let us boldly follow where the saints have trod.
> We are not divided, all one body we,
> one in hope and doctrine, one in charity.
> Onward Christian soldiers, marching as to war,
> with the cross of Jesus going as before."

In a world ripped apart by one religion waging war upon another, such imagery seems bizarre if not downright evil.

SEPTEMBER 26

Christianity is being divided into two camps, I think. They have really nothing to do with denominations or cultural traditions and everything to do with how we understand reality. One camp continues to be convinced that our understanding of God is the same "yesterday, today and forever". These are folk who remain certain that the ancient ways of understanding God are no different that the way we are to understand God today. This camp is not just filled with Biblical literalists or hierarchical traditionalists. It is filled with folk like us, folk who are often too afraid of the slippery slope. Folk who don't want to consider how God could be the same after the holocaust or after 9-11 or after a child is kidnapped, raped and killed. Simple answers that no longer work for the rest of us continue to shape and control this group.

The other camp is trans-denominational. It is not controlled by a fear of the slippery slope. It is willing to risk the questions, the re-imagining, indeed the very death of old ways of understanding God in order that something new can be brought to life. "See, I am doing a new thing." This camp is, I believe, the legitimate heir of Jesus' teachings. This camp seeks to continue the radical tradition of Jesus…of questioning authority, welcoming outsiders, challenging assumptions. Realistically, it didn't sell well in Jesus' time and it probably won't sell too well today. But so be it. This is the beginning of a new thing.

SEPTEMBER 27

E. Forrester Church is a good name for a pastor and that is precisely who he is. In his little book, "Everyday Miracles", Pastor Church offers a helpful image. In response to the question, "How does God answer prayer?" Church writes this: "God's answer is not a what or a how or a when or a why but a yes. Choose life and trust life. Grow in service and love. Take nothing for granted. Be thankful for the gift. Suffer well. Dare to risk much. Consecrate your world with laughter and with tears. And know not what I am or who I am or how I am, know only that I am with you."

SEPTEMBER 28

We have a religion that is rooted in thanksgiving. The greatest gift of Jesus, despite what some would tell us, is the gift of gratitude. Gratitude for life, for creation, for the privilege of being loved and loving others, for the joy of breathing in each new day, for the utter pleasure of knowing that we are cherished, imperfect, inadequate, insufficient as we may be. When Jesus welcomed the sinners to his table, he welcomed all of creation to share in the joy of being with God, entering into the kingdom of heaven. As our world reacts to the heinous crime of September 11th, it is vital that we who claim to be followers of Jesus remember what we are called to do, always and ever. It is a Christian duty, in times of peace and in times of war, to offer our gratitude. For our lives to be sure, for the safety of our family, of course, but also to give thanks that this may be a time for us to offer a hurting world a reason for hope, that this may be a time when we will have the opportunity to practice what we have for so long preached, that this may be a time when we can announce boldly and clearly what we really believe.

SEPTEMBER 29

Over the years, I have had a growing awareness that the God out there is no more. A God who sits somewhere on a heavenly throne nonchalantly deciding who wins and who loses, who gets well and who dies, who oppresses and who is oppressed, who goes to heaven and who goes to hell has diminished into nothingness for me. In its place is another image of the eternal God. It is of a God who is not out there somewhere but all around us. I am well aware that the Bible speaks of God as being out there, even up there, but it also, more often than you might imagine, envisions a God who is immediately present in and around us. "The whole earth is full of God's glory" is how Isaiah says it.

SEPTEMBER 30

I remember a time, long ago. I was visiting my grandparents on their parsonage farm in northeastern Nebraska. It was Saturday night and my "Opa" took my hand and led me to the church that he served next door to the farm house. We stood in the little narthex, no bigger than a not so big kitchen. He led me to a little closet-like door to the right. Upon opening the door I was surprised to see nothing more than a big hemp rope hanging. I stepped closer and looked up in awe as I saw how the rope was attached to a huge metal bell suspended high above us. Opa put my hands around the rope and together we pulled and were pulled as the bell peeled its one note song. Later I learned that this was a Saturday evening ritual, announcing for miles around that tomorrow is Sunday and Sunday is a different day. Sunday is for church.

We live in a very different time now. Not necessarily better. Not necessarily worse. Different. Sundays for most folk don't include church. I suppose if we decided to ring a bell every Saturday night it wouldn't be long before someone would sue us for breaching their peace. Nevertheless, there are some of us still who sense the need every week to set time aside to worship the creator, to ponder the sheer pleasure of just being alive and maybe even to offer a thank you or two.

OCTOBER 1

The gifted Anne Lamott is one of my favorite teachers. I turn to her writings often when I find myself in need of down home practical spiritual guidance and boy does she deliver! She describes herself as "a bad born-again Christian." which may give you a hint of why I like her so much. In a lecture of hers recently, she ruminated on what makes for good writing and she offered this quote: "The soul rejoices in hearing what it already knows." That is my sense of understanding the death of Jesus. My soul rejoices in hearing what it already knows…that a god who demands human sacrifice is a god I don't wish to know let alone worship. What my soul already knows is that in Jesus I have a window to the divine and that window is shaped by compassion, that window is designed by love.

OCTOBER 2

This from Robert Bolt via Sir Thomas More in "A Man For All Seasons":

"There comes a time in a man's life when he holds himself like water and if we let go, we never get it back."

What greater despair could there be than to realize at the end of one's time that we failed to stand up for what we believe? These are the times that define who we really are. These are the times that show the world what it means to be a follower of Jesus. The temptation to put other philosophies above our faith in a God of love is enormous right now. Certainly we can differ about how best to be compassionate and caring but we cannot claim to be Christians without that care and compassion.

OCTOBER 3

If Christianity is nothing but an ancient story, confined to history books and antiquated hymns then I'm not much interested in it.

I grew up in L.A. the city where nothing surprises. Easter services were often marked by dramatic displays of actors playing the resurrected Jesus and the astonished disciples and angels floating across sanctuaries on high wires while the USC marching band accompanied the two million voice choir. I can't think of anything more antithetical to the story from Mark than those kinds of ridiculous displays. It is precisely that kind of shoddy business that emerges out of our fear. We want to describe exactly how this resurrection business takes place. We want to assign the parts and make the costumes and control the lines. We want to get as far away from what Easter really means as we can.

OCTOBER 4

What does it mean to call Jesus the Son of God? In Nazareth, where Jesus grew up, it means he will be rejected by his own people, ridiculed by the local residents. And don't think for a moment that such rejection was because the Nazarenes were dumb or mean-spirited or whatever. The Son of God isn't recognized by the very people who know him best! You don't think that has powerful ramifications for the church, for we who claim to know Jesus best?

If that isn't enough we can turn to the very center of the gospel, Mark 8: 31. This is the heart of Mark's gospel, both literally and figuratively. Peter has just declared that Jesus is the Christ and all his buddies are congratulating him on what a smart disciple he is. But then Jesus describes what it means to be the Christ and he talks about being rejected and he talks about suffering and he talks about being killed and Peter will have none of it. And what does Jesus say? The harshest words anyone could utter about another. "Get behind me, Satan! For you are not on the side of God but of men." When, in our complacency, we convince ourselves that having power and privilege, riches and rewards, is what we get for being Christians, try remembering this little scene from Mark.

OCTOBER 5

When we gather up the names of those we want to pray for in worship, it isn't in order to convince God that they are worthy of being healed or helped but rather to express our love and concern for them and to ask others to share in that love and concern. Prayer becomes an opportunity to share our deepest desires, our highest hopes, with those we know will honor those hopes and desires and that honoring brings us closer to one another and thus closer to God.

What does it mean to pray? It is to enter deeply into the lives of others and to allow others to enter deeply into ours. This entrance is where God lives, the holy is found.

OCTOBER 6

There is a theory to, which I and others subscribe, that Jesus was once a disciple himself, a disciple of John the Baptist. It is, for me, a quite reasonable explanation for why John the Baptist figures so prominently in the beginning of all four gospels and yet disappears so quickly once Jesus' ministry begins.

John is confused about the rumors of Jesus as messiah. And who can blame him? John, like many of the faithful, was expecting a messiah that would bring cataclysmic change to the world order, who would topple the powers and turn pagan society on its ear. Like many Christians today, John the Baptist was an apocalyptic believer. He was convinced that the world was about to come to an end and the good guys rewarded and the bad guys damned. It's the kind of theology that can sell millions of books and be turned into multi-million dollar movies. It can make the cover of Time magazine and pack thousands into churches but, I submit, it isn't the theology of Jesus.

Oh, I think it was at one time. I think like many, many others, Jesus fell under the spell of John the Baptist and saw the value of his message with its call for dramatic personal change. But somewhere along the line Jesus decided that John's message and manner were limited, his ministry too narrow and so Jesus set off on his own, gathering up his own disciples, developing his own ministry, his own message.

OCTOBER 7

Why worship? William Willimon, a chaplain at Duke University, says that worship has a kind of uselessness about it. If we are in church on Sunday for a lecture or a performance or a pep rally, we'd best go elsewhere because none of these functions are at the heart of what we do on Sunday. He compares worship to a person running to meet her lover or a child dancing wildly about the room because the circus is in town. That's what worship is. And that is why it doesn't really make sense to those on the outside. A spring snowstorm had my wife and I confined to our home. Making the best of a potentially very romantic situation, we watched Franco Zefferelli's wonderful rendition of "Romeo and Juliet". I was especially struck by the kissing between those two star-crossed lovers. There was some really great kissing. Juliet giggled as she kissed her Romeo and the giggling sounded for all the world like the natural melody of a songbird. That is what worship, real worship should be like. Useless in the eyes of the world, essential for those in love.

OCTOBER 8

I am drawn to the Impressionists. To Manet and Monet, to Cezanne and Degas, to Paul Gauguin and Georges Seurat, to Renoir and, of course, Van Gogh. Now I very much appreciate some of the other schools. I can spend whole afternoons studying the 18th century Italian artists like Pannini and Guardi whose depictions of life in the 1700s is fascinating and highly realistic. I am enamored with the fine details that fill their canvasses. I am awed by their skill and humbled by their techniques but it is to the Impressionists that I turn for real inspiration. It is this same bias that informs my interpretation of scripture, my understanding of worship, my allegiance to the life and teachings of Jesus and certainly my tenuous grasp on the mystery and meaning of Easter.

OCTOBER 9

99.5% of us are Christians because we were raised in a primarily Christian world. Had we been born in Tokyo or Bangladesh we would more than likely be Buddhist or Hindu. Someone said to me recently: "If we believe that then what's so special about Christianity?" It is special because it shows those of us born in this world the path of compassion. Judaism is special when it does the same. Buddhism is special when it does the same. Islam is special when it does the same and on and on and on. What matters to me and thousands of other progressive Christians is the action of compassion. This we believe is the very presence of the kingdom of God. Whether it is manifested by Christian theology or some other theology does not matter. Compassion matters. I'll ask again what I've asked before: Why must Christianity be the only true religion? Why must there be one winner and all the rest losers?

Doesn't sound much like Jesus to me.

OCTOBER 10

I have long struggled with the church's insistence that the truth of Christianity must be transmitted using ancient creeds and archaic worldviews. We all can see where that has led us. There is an enormous split in Christianity that has divided us into two significant and very different camps. On the one hand are those good and faithful folk who refuse to jettison any of the images and language of another time and another culture. They continue to use words and symbols that no longer mean what they once meant. They ignore the movement of history, the revelations of science and technology, the incredible ramifications of a world that grows smaller everyday. It doesn't take too many contacts with non-Christians be they Jews, Muslims, Hindus, Buddhists…whatever, to come to the realization that there are folk outside of our own narrow understanding of the work and will of God who share our same fundamental values, our same desire for peace, our same longing for meaning. To continue to view the rest of the world from the extreme isolation of 1ˢᵗ century Palestine seems absurd at best and foolish to be sure.

OCTOBER 11

Radical egalitarianism was at the heart of early Christianity. According to Acts, the early church shared equally with everyone. When a disciple needed to be replaced they cast lots rather than held elections. Everyone was treated the same. No papal thrones or bishop miters, no pastoral robes or holy presiders. That all came later. That all came later after Jesus came and went.

OCTOBER 12

My mom used to use a wooden spoon to coax her ingredients together. Such an implement was also used on my much younger behind to force me into line. It's an approach that I haven't found all that useful either in child raising or Christian living.

To frighten folk into submission or to threaten them with punishment seems a strange way to witness to the love of God.

I've long held the belief that you can't make anyone believe anything. Oh, you can make them say they believe this or have faith in that but ultimately forcing people to faith always fails. I am Lutheran enough to believe that conversion is always the arena of God. We are called to live out lives that give evidence to what we believe. Our hope is that such a witness is so attractive that others will discover the joy we share in following Jesus. In the short run, such a model of faith is often less than productive. A huge dose of guilt or fear may produce Day Camp teachers or pot-luck participants but I doubt it does much in the way of real Christian growth or spiritual maturity. Of course, I'm tempted to pull out the wooden spoon around the time of our stewardship drives...

OCTOBER 13

For Jesus the kingdom comes in the now as well as the not yet. Over and over again, Jesus speaks of the kingdom being in our midst, in every act of kindness, in every gesture of grace. Each time we forgive, the kingdom comes. Each time we love our neighbor or our enemy or ourselves, the kingdom comes. Each time we welcome the stranger, feed the hungry, liberate the oppressed, serve the poor, work for peace and justice, the kingdom comes, the kingdom comes, the kingdom comes.

OCTOBER 14

"Whoever is not against us is for us." Can that possibly mean that the Jew at the food bank, the Muslim in the military, the atheist in the classroom…these people are for us? Can it be that the Iraqi who offers a cup of water to the thirsty is for us? It can if we free ourselves of thinking that Christianity is the only way into the kingdom of God. It can if we stop thinking of Jesus as some kind of ancient TV evangelist trying to convert the heathen. Despite what many in Christianity would have us believe, Christianity isn't about believing the right things. It isn't even about accepting Jesus as your personal savior. It certainly isn't about going to heaven on a guaranteed ticket. It's about a cool cup of water. It's about healing a broken world. It's about welcoming the stranger. It's about seeing others not as potential enemies but as potential friends.

OCTOBER 15

We all have heard, read or seen stories that show how compassion can bridge the gap of hatred and misunderstanding. Children brought together in upstate New York from both sides of the Middle East war and within days they are playing together, sharing not just meals but hopes and dreams of a different future. Nothing, I believe, is more powerful than compassion. It is what prevents some people from being eaten up by hate or envy or prejudice.

And yet despite our knowledge of its power, despite the proclamation of its truth by Jesus, we Christians have so often failed to employ it. Church history is filled with horrific examples of our inability to be compassionate...the Crusades, the Inquisition, our own Lutheran complicity in the Holocaust, the list is long and sobering and it always begins and ends with our failure to be compassionate.

OCTOBER 16

Anyone who has spent time reading Luther's voluminous works (50 some books in all) knows that he was a complicated and sometimes confused pastor. But everyone would agree that he was passionate! Right or wrong, Luther often forged ahead not particularly concerned with who he would offend or who he would appease. One of the great tragedies of contemporary Christianity, it seems to me, is we have lost that passion. We have been guided not so much by what ignites the fire among us but fear of what the flames might do. Too many of us in church leadership worry more about who we might offend rather than what we are called by our reformation tradition to do.

OCTOBER 17

One of the great advances in biblical scholarship in the last two hundred years or so is the realization that a culture's context has enormous influence on how the Bible was written and how the Bible is understood. I read recently one author's wish that just once when he sees those signs at football games that say "John 3:16" or whatever he would see one that says, "Read the Bible contextually!" To take a passage out of its context and assume it can stand entirely on its own is not just foolish and poor scholarship but downright dangerous. And yet this is one of Christianity's most common practices. I submit you can find justification for just about any human action, good or bad in the Bible. What matters, it seems to me, is the need to find out what is going on in the writer's mind as he records a particular event, saying or story. To honor the Bible's place in Christianity or Judaism is to first understand why, when and how a particular passage was written.

OCTOBER 18

Throughout his ministry, Jesus reaches out to those who can't reach back. Throughout his ministry, Jesus spends his time with the outsiders, the dispossessed, the poor and impoverished. He went from town to town and begged from others. He so identified with the poor that he became poor himself. And he became poor not because poverty is inherently good, anyone who has traveled in the Third World knows that isn't true, but because he believed that no one should ever be left behind. Not widows, not orphans, not heretics, not enemies, no one.

OCTOBER 19

One of my favorite authors, Ann Lamott, says there are really just two kinds of prayer: Helpmehelpmehelpme and Thankyouthankyouthankyou.

I'm not so sure about her theology with the first but I am committed to living by the second.

Each morning as I enter into consciousness I try to make my very first thought a line from the 118th Psalm, "This is the day the Lord has made let us rejoice and be glad in it." Some days are easier than others but every day holds the promise of opportunities for thanksgiving. Lying in bed and slowly becoming aware of the awakening of my body, slower and slower as the years go by, offers a sense of wonder and awe over the very gift of life.

Most mornings I sit and meditate for twenty minutes focusing on my breath, marveling that such a simple action as breathing can be such a source of thankfulness. A cup of coffee sipped in the shadow of our beautiful mountains puts perspective to my day and gratitude in my life.

"Benedictus," sang Zechariah. "Benedictus," I breathe in and out. Blessed be the Lord, for God looks favorably upon the people.

OCTOBER 20

It really is a considerate act to provide your loved ones with the details of your departing ceremony. Be specific. Tell your folks what music you want played or what poems you want read. It's been my experience that there is a lot of needless worrying over what the dead would want done. Save your family some trouble by pointing out precisely what you'd like to see...even though you probably won't be seeing too precisely by that point.

OCTOBER 21

Jesus, you may remember, ended up on a cross, a failure, a flop. In these times when anyone who doesn't speak of total victory is seen as slightly traitorous, any image of God that doesn't have us coming out on top isn't any image of God we want. And yet for two thousand years now, Christians who are willing to take great risks have discovered that following Jesus to the cross is precisely the image of God that brings victory. Over and over again, examples are offered of men and women who have chosen love over hate, sacrifice over selfishness, giving over getting and over and over again they have discovered the depth and richness that life can offer. Over and over again, they have discovered the truth that out of this kind of death of self comes a resurrection that unites us to all others, even those who would seek to destroy us.

OCTOBER 22

Surely the time has come to recognize that good, decent, seeking people just like us exist in Iran or Tokyo or New Delhi and that they are just as much children of the same loving God as are we. If God has chosen to reveal God's self to them in other ways than we have experienced, why must we continue to resent it, or worse, damn it? Could it not be that there are other ways to God than ours?

OCTOBER 23

Much of the language of Christianity is archaic. It confuses not just those on the outside looking in but many practicing Christians as well. One need only glance at the traditional creeds of the church to see what I mean. "I believe in God, the father almighty…" is how our most common creed begins and with it comes the immediate problem of anthropological imagery. Do we really think that God is male? Do we actually imagine that the divine has the physical characteristics of a man or even worse, the stunted psychological traits of most of us men? Of course not and yet we continue to employ symbols such as these in our futile quest to describe and thus contain God. Indeed, this very limited masculine description for God has given birth to entire theological systems that have managed to actually convince the believers that not only is God a male but maleness actually matters. The absurdity of denying the priesthood to women is but one ugly ramification of the misuse of language.

OCTOBER 24

I believe that following Jesus brings meaning to my life. I suspect that this statement, more than any other, including any statements I can make about God, is at the heart of my own spirituality. I believe that in following Jesus I discover a way of understanding life that enriches and invigorates my very being. Quite frankly, the intricate arguments over if, when and how, Jesus managed to become God hold only intellectual interest for me. The detailed descriptions that fill volumes of doctrine, both ancient and modern, matter little to me. I certainly appreciate the work that has gone into the formation of our Christian faith but when that faith forgets that at its heart is the life and teachings of Jesus, I will, I hope always, reject the faith.

OCTOBER 25

I have long said that if you want to know what a person believes, look at their life. See what they spend their money on, how they treat their families, how they view the poor or the outcast. It may also be revealing to take a look at what they sing. Several years ago I was asked to be a speaker at a retreat for a congregation in Colorado Springs. Just as I arrived they were engaged in a hymn sing led by a big burly guy whose cheeks were dripping with tears as he guided them through one sentimental favorite after another. "Music has the power to sooth the savage breast" and it was certainly doing that as I walked in. I sat and listened for a while, trying to get a sense of my soon to be audience. It was disconcerting to say the least. I soon came to realize that I was either the right man at the wrong time or the wrong man at the right place. Because we were talking a different language, we were singing different tunes, we were, I believe, worshipping different gods.

OCTOBER 26

The first proposition of the new Christianity is that God can no longer be understood as a Being. That a God who somehow resides out beyond the stars, sitting on a heavenly throne and cavalierly deciding what will be and what will not is untenable and unbelievable. So what do we put in its place? Must we deny all supernatural forces in creation? Is the only option atheism, a complete absence of something divine? I think not but I turn to you and to others to help us discover how we are to understand the divine without accepting a divine being.

A second proposition is to consider that Jesus' ministry on earth was not part of some pre-arranged plan but a living out of what Jesus understood to be a holy life. His actions toward the poor, his stories of grace, his eating and drinking with so-called sinners, was his attempt to show the world what really mattered. Stunningly, this attempt was quickly diminished as Christianity developed not around the life of Jesus but around his death. It soon mattered far less to follow Jesus than to believe what others said about Jesus.

Those are two good questions for us to struggle with. And let us take our leadership here from the world of science that welcomes the struggle because they recognize within it the ongoing search for greater truth. An authentic scientist is unafraid of having his or her assumptions questioned because he or she knows there is a greater good to be attained. We should do no less.

OCTOBER 27

I think it was the first year I was living in the Rockies that Bob Reedy, a mentor of mine and so many others, stopped me as we were walking down a aspen-filled trail out behind his house. He pointed up at a beautiful red-tailed hawk circling overhead. "Anytime you happen to see a hawk or an eagle, see them as symbols of God and a call to prayer." For over twenty years I've remembered his words and, most of the time, I've obeyed them.

OCTOBER 28

"Just to be is a blessing. Just to live is holy." This is the prayer of Rabbi Abraham Heschel, one of the great spiritual leaders of Judaism. Please forgive me for belaboring a point but this is, again, the message of Jesus. This is what compels him to reach out to the outcast, feed the hungry, serve the poor and, yes, love his enemies. If life is precious, if it really is holy and a blessing, then we as followers of Jesus are graced with the good fortune to follow in the savior's footsteps, to do as he did, to go where he went, to love as he loved. If life is precious, if it really is holy and a blessing, then we as followers of Jesus are graced with the good fortune to feed the hungry, serve the poor, love our enemies. This is grace. This is what we are thankful for.

OCTOBER 29

"Be not afraid."

Such a radical understanding of grace allows us to venture places we have been told not to go, to explore areas that were once forbidden. It wasn't all that long ago, some of us remember, that African-American people were deemed less than equal in the eyes of many Christians, which means, of course, in the eyes of their God as well. But somewhere along the line, insightful people, brave people, grace-filled people, began to explore Jesus' image of the kingdom, his understanding of grace in ways that the church had forbidden. Over time, others joined the exploration, emboldened by the freedom that amazing grace allows and soon leaves were added to the table welcoming folk of different color, different cultures, different sexual orientation, different beliefs. It is a crazy, chaotic mix to be sure but it is, I believe the kind of hospitality revealed by Jesus. The God of my continuing reformation puts no strings on grace...none.

Such an understanding, of course, has profound impact on other aspects of the faith. The church, for one. A church that witnesses to the unconditional love of God by welcoming all shapes and sizes of God's children is bound to look pretty weird. Unanimity of thought takes a fall when freedom to think and believe for oneself enters the equation. So why have a community of faith at all? Why not encourage folk to just do their own thing on their own time in their own way. For me there is something holy about community. Something sacred happens when people gather together to share in each others' lives, to admit faults and failures, to join together in a meal, no matter how simple. Once again, I'm not so certain that we all have to believe the same way to experience this holy thing. Quite frankly, I'm not all that interested in being with folk who all look the same way or act the same way or think the same way as I do and I suspect you wouldn't either.

OCTOBER 30

"For God so loved the world that He gave…" Love and giving go hand in hand. It is the very core of our faith, encapsulated by that most famous of verses. It has been of more than passing interest to me to observe so many relationships that have failed to grasp this eternal truth. When our love is separated from our willingness to give, it quickly withers and dies. To love is to open ourselves, to give up the protective shell that shields us from the passions of others. The person unwilling or unable to let go of such self security is the person most to be pitied because it is the person incapable of love. The central symbol of Christianity is the cross, a powerful sign of how we understand love and a disturbing reminder of where that love can take us.

OCTOBER 31

It was St. Augustine who said, "Thou has made us for thyself, O Lord, and our hearts are restless until they rest in thee." We are created to be in relationship with God. We are created to be loved by God and to love God in return. Jesus showed us how to experience that divine rest. It has little to do with intellectual assertions or theological presupposition and everything to do with simply following Him.

NOVEMBER 1

I would love to be able to say that the picture on the front page of the New York Times that showed Jewish, Muslim and Christian leaders, all decked out in their religious finery and gathered all together for a press conference in Jerusalem, was a hopeful symbol of religious toleration. It was, however, a symbol of just the opposite. The only reason these representatives of religions that seem to rarely come together came together was to denounce the planned Gay pride gathering scheduled for the summer in Jerusalem. They were united, I believe, not by any sense of searching for peace and justice in a troubled world but by their bigotry and prejudice. They were united by all that is wrong with religion today.

Some, of course, will say that they were united by faith, united by an image of God that is attested to in the Bible and described by thousands of years of tradition. And it is true that a strong case can be made for the condemnation of homosexuality in Christian, Jewish and Islamic scriptures. How often do we read or hear someone quoting a particular passage to justify their prejudice? And yet these same scriptures can be used to argue that inclusiveness and hospitality are commanded by God as well. Who is right here? Who is wrong? Should we add up all the verses for one particular side and declare a winner, declare God's final opinion?

If that is the route we choose, perhaps we had better spend a little time gathering some additional information.

For instance, we can begin with the overwhelming evidence that Abraham and thousands of other religious ancestors of ours were convinced that the God of Israel was but one of many gods occupying celestial space. The concept of one God alone is a relatively recent religious doctrine and certainly comes long after Moses brings down those Ten Commandments which include, of course, the acknowledgement in the very first line that other gods most certainly existed. Even the authors of the Hebrew Scriptures utilize distinctly different images and names for God, writing as they do centuries after the events they are describing. Which God are we quoting when we declare with such certainty that we speak for the divine?

NOVEMBER 2

"An inch of time cannot be bought by an inch of gold."

It is an ancient Chinese proverb that has great validity today. It is abundantly clear to me that nothing is cherished more in our current world than time...and nothing is more abused. We've all heard it from others, from ourselves. "I haven't any time!" The truth, of course, is that we all have the time, we just choose to use it in less than satisfying ways.

One of the gifts of Christ is a perspective on time. Nowhere in scripture will you find a sense of Jesus being harried by lack of time. He uses his time by giving it to others. Over and over again, Jesus speaks of the joy of service, the joy of sacrificing for others, the joy of loving others...indeed it is the very reason we have time according to the gospel...to give it away.

NOVEMBER 3

"The word of the Lord was rare in those days," it says in I Samuel. For many of us it may seem that way today. But perhaps it is because we have been looking for it in the wrong places. Understanding Jesus less as mighty messiah and more as lowly outsider may allow us the joy of discovering that the word of the Lord isn't rare at all, its just been hidden for a time, hidden behind a conspiracy of silence.

NOVEMBER 4

You've seen it. A football player makes it into the end zone and falls to his knees or points to the sky in a moving declaration of his faith. "Thank you, Jesus!"

I humbly suggest that if this is indeed what the player is proclaiming, he has both misread scripture and misunderstood Jesus. More in keeping with the gospel would have the player who just got slammed to the ground in a fifteen-yard loss and then subjected to piling on by the defense slowly emerge from the bottom of the human heap and point his finger skyward. "Thank you, Jesus!" he could correctly claim as he limped back to the huddle. I'm not being entirely facetious here. Such an image is, I am convinced, more in keeping with what it means to declare Jesus as the Son of God than all the exuberant rituals in end zones combined.

NOVEMBER 5

Does prayer change things? Absolutely! I see evidence of it all the time. Evidence in lives that enrich and reward one another. Evidence in acts of compassion and mercy. Evidence as together we work for justice for all people. Prayer has enormous power but I don't think it is found in pious pleadings or magical incantations. It is found as we continue to commit our lives to the vision given to us by Jesus, a vision that turned old ways of thinking upside down, a vision that shocked some and outraged most others but a vision that continues to offer guidance and hope to folk like us as we seek to reconstruct Christianity into what it was always intended to be.

NOVEMBER 6

Too many of us Christians have decided we'd rather stick with John the Baptist than Jesus of Nazareth. We rather like the idea of blasting away at all those who don't believe the way we do. We kind of get off on calling our opponents broods of vipers and hordes of villains. Some Christians, I dare say, rub their hands in glee as they imagine certain hated folk (usually other Christians, by the way) spending eternity tossing and turning in the unquenchable fires of hell.

I had a confirmation pastor a little like that. He used to spend inordinate amounts of time lecturing us all on who was damned and who was saved. I was sort of a slow learner so it took me a little longer to realize that all the people who were going to be saved thought just like my pastor and all who weren't didn't. Somewhere along the line I came to the startlingly existential realization that if heaven meant spending time with people like Pastor Anderson, I'd just as soon choose the alternative.

NOVEMBER 7

We really are odd ducks, we Christians. The world looks at us not so much with disdain as disinterest. "Get real" is the suggestion offered frequently especially in these troubling, terrifying days. I can't tell you how many times in recent months people have told me that what Jesus taught doesn't apply today. This is the real world, Rich! But, you see, this is the real world for me and, I pray, for many of you. This is what really matters…giving our lives to God, serving the poor and the helpless, reaching out to reconcile ourselves to our enemies, recognizing that money really doesn't bring happiness…this is what is real! Worship should constantly seek to express that reality and we do it in ways that may seem strange to others but point to ultimate reality for us. It is the ultimate reality of love and grace and forgiveness and acceptance. The ultimate reality we call God.

NOVEMBER 8

Jesus says to the woman "Your faith has made you well." Jesus says to the parents whose little girl has died, "Don't be afraid only believe." In what? The Athanasian Creed? The Augsburg Confession? What faith can that poor woman have had? In "the one, holy, catholic and apostolic church"? Of course not. They simply trusted Jesus. They simply trusted that the image, the impression, of God that Jesus was evoking by his actions and words was one they could give their hearts to, one that they could give their lives to.

NOVEMBER 9

The hallmark of Christianity should be the willingness to follow the compassionate life as modeled by Jesus. If a born and bred Lutheran wants to do that, fine. If a Methodist wants to do that, great. If an agnostic or even an atheist wants to give it a try, come on down! Belief should not be a barrier to the compassionate life. In Matthew, Mark and Luke, Jesus rarely says: "Believe me". What he does say, over and over again, is: "Follow me." You don't have to be a Lutheran to do that.

(Footnote: Please understand that this in no way denigrates either Lutheranism or Christianity. The Lutheran tradition has been a rich and wonderful resource for the Christian movement. I cherish my heritage, particularly its legacy of intellectual inquiry and reformation, but I am unconvinced that all folk are meant to be Lutherans just as I am unconvinced all folk are meant to be Christian. I am convinced that all folk are meant to be loved and cherished by the spirit of God.)

NOVEMBER 10

Let's assume that Jesus came not two thousand years ago but thirty years ago. Not in the time of Pontius Pilate and Herod the Great but Richard Nixon and Nikita Kruschev. Not when the world was thought to be flat and the heavens a celestial umbrella but after Columbus, after Sir Issac and Professor Einstein. Not when appeasing God meant sacrificing animals or even human beings but after the Holocaust, after Hiroshima, after My Lai. What language would you use, what symbols would you employ to tell the Good News? What ways would you find to proclaim your faith in a God of love who became a man of flesh? Would you choose an angel's visitation and a virgin birth? Would such an image be effective in sharing the truth? Would you tell of water being changed into wine or Lazarus walking out of his smelly tomb? Would there be demands to be washed in the blood of the lamb or invitations to eat and drink flesh and blood?

NOVEMBER 11

Mary Magdalene has long been identified as the prostitute who changed her ways for Jesus. But, in fact, there is no Biblical evidence that Mary Magdalene was ever a prostitute or a person of ill repute. Luke alone tells us she was healed of seven demons but as to what those demons were or what they represented, he and everyone else has been silent. There is a tradition that Mary Magdalene was the woman who washed the feet of Jesus as he began his final days in Jerusalem. Some folks believe that Mary Magdalene is the sister of Martha whose brother Lazarus Jesus raised from the dead. All kinds of traditions have emerged around this enigmatic woman. Some, and I underscore some, have even hypothesized that Mary was the wife of Jesus and they base this proposition on some rather intriguing evidence. What I find so fascinating about Mary is the prominence she seems to have throughout both the references in the Bible and in tradition. Mary Magdalene. Mary from the town of Magdala. Only there is a slight problem here. No one has ever found any reference that can authentically verify a real town called Magdala. It is not mentioned in Hebrew scriptures or in the writings of Josephus, a historian of the time. Some scholars have suggested that it is actually a derivation of the Hebrew word magdal which means great or large. Mary Magdalene may actually mean Mary the Great. Hmmmm.

NOVEMBER 12

I don't know if this happens to anyone else but every morning when I stumble into the bathroom and look into the mirror to see if I am still here, I encounter the same guy each time. I squint at my reflection and there I still am…the same as I've always been. What I see is what I remember seeing in High School, the same puss that was there in college and all through the '60s and every decade since. Same guy smiling back at me each day. Amazing thing. Not too long ago, I was talking to a friend of mine who is in his mid-eighties and he says the same. He looks in the mirror and sees a kid from the great depression all bright-eyed and bushy-tailed. My suspicion is that this is some kind of holy gift from God and not discernible by anyone else because if you were to look at my friend what you would probably see is a handsome but shriveled up face with white hair on top and lots of years in between. And, I dare say, even with me, were you to draw near and stand as close as my bathroom mirror you might meditate over how many high school kids you know who have graying temples, wrinkling skin and the total absence of abdominal muscle tone.

But that's the way it is with God. God knows that confronting all those rapidly passed years the very first thing each morning would be a terrible way to start the day and so, in divine love, God gives us this wonderful little heavenly gift from the bathroom mirror as a gentle, holy way of getting us going again. By grace are we saved.

NOVEMBER 13

"For God so loved the world…" for what? So he could rain fire and brimstone down on it? You can see the danger of this kind of thinking. It demeans creation. It makes our spiritual lives more important than our physical lives and I defy anyone to defend that position from the life and teachings of Jesus…especially in this gospel of Luke. Jesus reaches out to the lepers and heals them. Why? Why not let them suffer with their skin disease since the world's going to come to an end anyway. Jesus ate with the sinners and became defiled and unclean according to religious law. Why risk it? Why didn't he make sure he was pure and sinless if the world was about to come to an end? Over and over again, we have examples of Jesus entering into the world not escaping from it. This is the model for Christians then and now. It is the reason we have built hospitals and colleges, sent millions and millions of dollars to fight hunger and poverty, sought peaceful settlements to conflicts and worked for justice for all people. We do this not because the world doesn't matter and its all going to come to an end anyway. We do this because this is what Jesus called us to do. "Go and do likewise." he said. Go and do likewise

NOVEMBER 14

Whether we like it or not, and the disciples certainly did not, Jesus stands with the outsiders. Jesus can be found, over and over again, with those who are considered dumb or damned, unclean or uncouth. To follow Jesus then is to be unconcerned with orthodox belief and totally consumed with welcoming the unorthodox. What does that mean? Stop for a minute and think who, of all people, you would not want to be sitting next to right now. That's the one that Jesus welcomes. Imagine a congregation filled with the very people you'd like the world to be emptied of and that's where you'll find Jesus. Are they Muslims? Are they gay? Are they Republicans? Are they atheists? There's Jesus. There's Jesus. There's Jesus.

NOVEMBER 15

To be compassionate is to enter into the lives of our enemies. It is to ask ourselves what we would do in the same circumstances. It is to become the Muslim father seeking to honor tradition and yet live in the 21st century. It is to enter into the life of the young woman who has been raised to revere modesty in a way that seems both archaic and offensive to us but holy to her. It is to really experience the hopelessness of a teenage boy on the West Bank who sees no future, no hope, no purpose. It is to weep with the Israeli parent whose child has been blown to smithereens by a suicide bomber. Compassion has a power to bind us to others as nothing else can. It has the power to transcend foreign cultures and unknown traditions. It is the only force active in the world today that can bring peace to our world.

I know how naïve that sounds. I know how quickly we can dismiss such talk as just the expected pious pap from the preacher. But I wonder if there really is any other way? Isolation is no longer an option. Violence may solve matters in the short term but never for long. What else can there be but a radical attempt at compassion?

NOVEMBER 16

Gene Robinson is an openly gay man who has been elected by the people of his diocese and confirmed by the national Episcopal convention to serve as Bishop of New Hampshire. The Anglican Communion, which consists of participants and descendents of the Church of England around the world, is in turmoil over Gene. In an extraordinary convocation, Anglican bishops from all over the world converged in London to discuss the ramifications of having Gene Robinson as a bishop. Cries from conservative church leaders warned of the threat to the unity of the church. Some bishops proclaimed that they would not recognize Robinson as a legitimate church leader; others spoke openly of leaving the Anglican Communion if this "sexual pervert" is allowed to be consecrated.

A most interesting threat coming as it does from bishops who are part of a church that was initially formed, in part, because of the rather unusual sexual desires of the King of England.

We heard these same outcries from many of the same people thirty years ago when Episcopalians began ordaining women. "It will split the church!" they cried. "It goes against the Bible!" they claimed. Indeed, church history buffs will recall that the same threats were made when Christians in America forced their churches to reject slavery and to treat every human being as a child of God.

NOVEMBER 17

We don't know for sure if we are interpreting the Bible correctly. Continuing discoveries in archaeology, science, anthropology, linguistics and more call us to constantly reevaluate our prior assumptions about a particular passage in the Bible. An obvious but still good example would be the scientific discoveries that have determined the earth's age and development. Seeing evidence that the world evolved over millions of years had serious biblical scholars reexamining their understanding of the first chapter of Genesis. Was this a literal description of the creation of the world or a poetic one? Was it intended to be a scientific description or a theological position? Although there are still some folk who deny the overwhelming evidence, one can see how such scientific data demands a reassessment of biblical interpretation. It is helpful to remember that Jesus himself would have assumed, as everyone else in his day did, that the world was flat, the earth was the center of the universe and heaven resided just a few feet past that last star. We now know that the cosmos goes on into infinity. Such a realization had better have us questioning what it means to point up to the sky to indicate God's place of residence.

NOVEMBER 18

Jesus had, I firmly believe, no intention of building a church foundation or blue-printing an economic system. He wasn't a church planner. He wasn't a burgeon-ing CEO. He was a radical Jewish prophet who reminded people of what they didn't want to hear…that the God they worshipped was a God of love who bore no favorites but had a decided bias for the poor.

NOVEMBER 19

Many years ago, we lived in Cedar Rapids, Iowa. A different place, I dare say, from Summit County, Colorado. As one who loves to eat and eat well, Summit County with its over 100 restaurants is my own little piece of heaven. Cedar Rapids, on the other hand, well…let's just say continental cuisine wasn't a high priority back then. However, it did have a little Greek restaurant that I came to love. Unpretentious, quite reasonable with some of the best souvlaki this side of Athens. Sue and I would often meet there for lunch and our late night dinners there were always something special. I don't ever recall having even a mediocre meal there. It was always a very pleasant experience. But it wasn't until I had visited there at least a dozen times that I happened to notice the theological significance of my dining pleasure. Just about the time I was reveling in my second cup of coffee and my third bite of divinely inspired cheesecake, the check would be discreetly placed near my elbow. Now usually this is our least enjoyable event of the evening but even this was handled in a way that made it not only more palatable but even fun. As I say, it took me about twelve times before I realized the religious significance of paying for my meal in this favorite Greek restaurant. Written boldly across the little tray that held my check was the word "Eucharisto!" Why I didn't notice it right away still baffles me but eventually even I was captured by my chef's theology. "Eucharisto!" It means, simply, "Thank you!" It comes from the same root word as what we use to describe Holy Communion: The Eucharist.

Now I don't know about you but every time I see the word "Eucharist" I am captured by that sense of joy and thanksgiving that I always associate with sharing in this holy sacrament. Seeing the word almost never fails to bring out a deep sense of gratitude from within. Whether I come across it in a worship bulletin, a textbook or the tray of a little Greek restaurant, I am reminded of the invitation to offer thanks for all that I have and all that I am. Eucharisto.

NOVEMBER 20

It is quite clear that those first Christians devoted themselves not to the acquisition of personal wealth or professional success. The Protestant work ethic that has all of us beaming with pride over how well we have done doesn't seem to play much of a role here. Rather what we have are people so committed to others that they are willing to "sell their possessions and goods and distribute to all, as any had need." Doesn't sound too American to me.

"From each according to their ability. To each according to their need." Remember that one? It's not from Jesus. It's from Karl Marx. Although I am a convinced capitalist, I think it instructive to remember that the early church was based on very different principles.

Could it be that part of the culture of deceit that so envelops Christianity takes its shape as we deny the very roots of our faith?

Does our reluctance to embrace this early Christian practice of radical generosity make it easier to fudge on other Christian principles as well?

NOVEMBER 21

"Let not your hearts be troubled." But we have so much to be troubled about. We can begin with terrorism but it certainly doesn't end there. Our hearts are troubled each week when the mortgage comes due or when out kids haven't made it home at their curfew. We're troubled every time we open up the paper and read the headlines. We're troubled in a myriad of troubling ways. How can Jesus say such a stupid thing?

"Believe in God, believe also in me." Over the years I've come to cherish the realization that, for me, Jesus is a window to God. If I want to understand what is holy in this life, what is sacred and true, I find that understanding in the life and teachings of this rabbi from Nazareth. Any image of God that is not in keeping with the spirit of Jesus is not a valid image for me. Such a realization provides enormous comfort. In my search for meaning, in my journey of faith, I have come to the conclusion that a rich and rewarding life can be mine as I walk the path of Jesus. In those moments when I love as he loved, when I forgive as he forgave, when I serve as he served, I experience the wonder of existence, I experience the kingdom of God, I experience the divine joy of having an untroubled heart.

NOVEMBER 22

I have never made a secret of the fact that the bodily resurrection of Jesus is not a requirement of my faith. The suspension of the laws of nature is not a requisite for my committing my life to Jesus. Not too long ago, someone gave me a book, written by a Lutheran pastor no less, whose premise was that the bones of Jesus were found in a cave somewhere in Palestine and the whole civilized world began crumbling down. Ultimately, a crusading Christian archaeologist proved that they really weren't the bones of Jesus and so Christianity could continue to flourish knowing that Jesus actually did shoot up into the heavens like a rocket ship. I'm told it sold a lot of copies. I wouldn't recommend it. Not just because it was poorly written but because it is based on a premise that I find not helpful for my own journey of faith.

Nevertheless, I am avidly, avowedly, convinced that the resurrection of Christ occurred and continues to occur. I see evidence of it all the time. Each time our eyes are opened to see suffering in the world and our call to serve those in need, there is resurrection, there is life out of death. Each time one of you recognizes the reality of the kingdom of God in your midst, there is resurrection. Each time we look with compassion upon those in need, each time we sacrifice our time and our possessions for others, each time we realize anew that God's love and grace is generated not just for us but for all the world, we encounter the resurrection, Christ rises again and again and again. So please don't tell me or others that I don't believe in the resurrection. It may be that our understanding of the term is different but I am as committed to my understanding as others are to theirs.

NOVEMBER 23

What do kings do when they're not opening up supermarkets? They conquer other countries, that's what they do! The symbol of Christ as King was, I suppose, an accurate image back when Christians spent most of their time and energy trying to convince others to be Christians too. We are certainly all aware that some of that convincing took some pretty awful forms. Of course there are many Christians, millions of Christians, I suppose, who do not share my conviction that such language is both archaic and inappropriate. On a recent trip to LA, I saw a bumper sticker advertising an upcoming event at a local church. It implored me to come to their "Crusade". Such language is more than a little inflammatory for the millions of Muslims who live in our country. I suspect, however, that the image of Christ as king resonates with the owner of that bumper sticker. It is, I propose, a perversion of a beautiful faith. I further propose that even we who claim to abhor such theology participate and support it when we continue to use language that no longer means what we intend it to mean.

NOVEMBER 24

Every time we put ourselves ahead of others, we announce to the world that we no longer are following Jesus. Every time we choose violence over compassion, hatred over love, exclusion over welcome, we turn our backs on Jesus. Whenever the church announces that it has the only way, whenever it refuses to feed the spiritually hungry, whenever it foolishly thinks that it and God are synonymous, it proclaims Christianity has nothing to do with Christ.

NOVEMBER 25

Jesus' primary purpose during his ministry was, I believe, to proclaim that the Kingdom of God was in our midst. That it was within our grasp and available for us to experience. But the Kingdom of God was not what people expected. It was not a world where everyone sat around playing harps and reclining on clouds. It was not a world where the good guys win and the bad guys burn. It was instead a world built on heavenly justice. It was a world where the poor and the outcast are blessed and the meek inherit everything. The kingdom of God is not a place where buildings don't fall down and thousands, even millions of innocent people aren't murdered. The kingdom of God is where we come together, across all boundaries and barriers, across all religions and cultures, and seek to serve the suffering, liberate the oppressed, and, yes, even love our enemies. We have, I am afraid, confused the Kingdom of God with our nice homes, our comfortable lives, our 2.5 kids upstairs safely tucked in their beds. Good and wonderful as those benefits are, it is very difficult to imagine Jesus calling them the kingdom of God. So when our way of life is threatened, when our comfort is attacked, we may need to remember that God is not absent from the kingdom. It may be us who have gone missing.

NOVEMBER 26

Isn't it time, indeed isn't it long past time, that we recognize the danger of assuming that there is one external, objective, revealed standard for ethical behavior for all time? Why must we continue to turn to a book that, at varying times, sanctified slavery, gave its blessing to barbarous acts, condemned women for speaking, let alone teaching, in church, and on and on and on, as the be all and end all of our ethical authority? Surely we all can see how dangerous such thinking is and where it can lead. "See, I am doing a new thing," and that new thing is not necessarily bound to even the Bible. This is dangerous territory, I know but it is vital, in a world that has religions hurling hate-filled passages from so-called holy books back and forth, for us to find ways of revelation outside the limitations of centuries-old conclusions.

NOVEMBER 27

One of the most influential theologians in my life is an ex-Dominican priest named Matthew Fox. The Roman Catholic Church has excommunicated him for his writings, which have only endeared him more to me. He is, of course, a radical and many others outside the Catholic Church criticize his theology as well but he has, for me, been an enormous help and a guiding light on my own journey of faith. In any case, one Sunday morning in San Francisco, Sue and I had the opportunity to worship at Grace Episcopal Cathedral on Nob Hill. It was tremendous worship, filled with music to inspire and words to disturb. Everything good worship should be. We were especially thrilled that at the Adult Sunday School class, Matthew Fox was the guest speaker. I couldn't wait to hear what he had to say and we raced to the basement to get a good seat. Here was a heretic of the finest order, a pilgrim on a path that often crossed with mine. So you can imagine my chagrin when the very first thing out of his mouth was how disappointed he was when, as a young priest back in '60s, the Latin mass was changed into the language of the people. "It lost so much" he said and I could hardly believe my Protestant ears. "The words now often get in the way of the message of God", he continued and I nearly fell off my chair. But as he went on and as I listened further I began to understand his disappointment. The perfectly understandable English of the mass diminished the mystery of the universe for Matthew Fox. It is an interesting critique and worth paying attention to. Too often, too much of religion expends energy trying to explain it all to our brains when what it should be doing is opening our eyes in awe.

NOVEMBER 28

"Lord bless our meal, and as you satisfy the needs of each of us, make us mindful of the needs of others."

And what, we must ask, are the needs of others?

There is no question that the attack in New York and Washington was the work of terrorists. But have there been other terrors perpetrated in the past and even now in the present that we have not responded to with the same noble vigilance that we now display? Are you aware, for instance, that 12 million children will die this year from hunger and preventable diseases? Imagine the terror that holds for a mother no different than you except that she is living in Africa or living in Afghanistan. Is that not a kind of terrorism? Someone told me this week that the equivalent of a fully loaded 747 goes down each day with third world women aboard. Killed by preventable diseases and malnutrition. Is that not a kind of terrorism? I confess to being somewhat stunned when well-intentioned folk wonder why Americans are so hated by some. Have we forgotten that we who are but 5% of the world's population and yet we produce 25% of the world's carbon dioxide emissions helping to choke this entire planet into extinction? Have we forgotten that we in America give but $30 per capita in developmental assistance to less fortunate citizens of this world? $30! Norway, for instance, gives $285 per capita. Nearly ten times the amount we sometimes grudgingly offer. Have we forgotten that 20% of the world can access only 5% of the world's meat and fish? "Lord bless our meal and as you satisfy the needs of each of us, make us mindful of the needs of others."

NOVEMBER 29

I worry that too many of our expressions, too much of our symbolism is steeped in a world view that no longer makes sense to people. The primitive Jewish notion of sacrifice and atonement so readily picked up by Paul and others in the early church makes little sense today. Talking or singing of a God who needs a human sacrifice is not only gross but entirely obfuscated from modern people. Does our very understanding of Jesus' death need reformation? I certainly believe it does. Does my need for reforming it mean that I dismiss or diminish it? I don't think so but it does mean I must be open to new insight, new wisdom that helps those of us not raised in a world where animal sacrifice was commonplace and Copernicus was yet to be born.

NOVEMBER 30

"Blessed are the poor," Jesus says. "Blessed are those who mourn. Blessed are the meek. Blessed are you when men revile you for my sake." Such foolishness. Such non-sense. Incomprehensible to those of us who, like Nicodemus, have not been born again.

I'd like to tell you about the time I was born again but it's hard to decide which of the 4,873 times would be most helpful. I suppose I could tell you about the time I was feeling sorry for myself…again…and found myself in the hospital visiting someone who really had reason for feeling sorry for herself but, oddly, she didn't. Instead, she spoke of the joy she had experienced in this life, the pleasure that had been hers as she raised her family and served her God. Nothing monumental, mind you, but a faithful willingness to offer herself to others. Now as she was nearing the end of her life, she looked back with tremendous satisfaction at the sacrifices she had made. Sacrifices that didn't seem like sacrifices at all, not to her. It was her offering. Such insight allowed for my being born again, again.

DECEMBER 1

Not long ago, I showed my afternoon group of pre-schoolers the animated movie, "The Prince of Egypt". It is the story of Moses and it includes the epic battle between Pharaoh and Moses that culminates with the slaughter of every first born child in Egypt. Curiously, we have no historical evidence that such a slaughter ever took place. Indeed, we have no archaeological evidence that the Hebrew people were ever in Egypt or if they were that they ever had an actual exodus out. Nevertheless, the story is part of our religious history and so we continue to teach it to our children. As I watched the portrayal of a dark spirit entering the homes of all those who didn't put the lamb's blood over their doors and thus were victims of infanticide, I wondered if this was an image of God that continues to be helpful. Judging from the reactions of the children, I think not. Dare we suggest that such a depiction is no longer valid? When I read of leaders in Israel and elsewhere, both political and religious, claiming that certain territories are their divine right to possess, no matter who dies, I think we dare and dare to do it soon.

DECEMBER 2

This one from Nathanial Hawthorne: "Time flies over us, but leaves its shadow behind."

What we do with whatever time we have is of great importance.

I love the little benediction from, I think, St. Augustine: "Life is short. There is not much time to gladden the hearts of others, so be swift to love, make haste to be kind."

God uses us, indeed God becomes us, when we realize the truth of this call. At our best, we are instruments of love, pathways of peace.

DECEMBER 3

Matthew and Luke were written some 60 years after the death of Jesus. In those intervening decades all kinds of stories surely circulated about Jesus. Discerning what is factual and what is not is both challenging and very rewarding. The gospel writers offer us clues to our quest. For instance, Matthew begins his beautiful book with a genealogy that attempts to trace Jesus all the way back to Abraham thus providing evidence that Jesus is indeed the long awaited Jewish messiah. Matthew does this by mentioning all the fathers from Abraham right down to Joseph. A very extensive list made all the more interesting when you read in the very next paragraph that Mary is conceived not by Joseph but by the Holy Spirit.

So why the genealogy?

If Joseph didn't have anything to do with the conception, why is Matthew making such a big deal of Jesus' roots? But there's even more here. In this extensive list of Daddies we can find four women duly noted.

What's that all about?

Well, let's look at the ladies. There is Tamar. You can read about her in Genesis 38. She's the one who dresses up as a prostitute and tricks a very important man into giving her some respectability. Then there is Rahab who dressed as a prostitute because she was one. There is Ruth who you can read about in the Book of Ruth. She is an outsider, a non-Jew. And finally there is Bathsheba. You remember her. She was the wife of Uriah, King David's general. But David took a liking to her and had Uriah sent to the front from which he never came back. Four women. All well known to Matthew's readers and all of dubious background. Very interesting.

DECEMBER 4

You know, of course, that Palestine in the time of Jesus was an occupied country, much as it is today. Only back then the occupiers were Romans. If you know anything about history, you know that occupying forces do some pretty terrible things. They take over homes. They blow up schools. They enslave or kill men. And they often rape the women. This has been shown quite terribly in our own lifetime. We remember with horror the stories out of Bosnia and Serbia. The Vietnam War left hundreds maybe thousands of mixed-race children in its wake. It is a horrible but very real casualty of occupation.

Consider this:…the scandal of Mary's pregnancy, that Joseph so nobly responds to, is not the result of a beatific blessing surrounded by cherubim and seraphim but the brutal rape by a Roman soldier.

DECEMBER 5

The word is "mamzer".

It is a Hebrew word that means "of questionable birth" or "illegitimate child". Some Bible scholars are suggesting that this is an accurate description of Jesus. They posit this thesis on some very intriguing evidence. A mamzer, you see, would be rejected in his own community, as Jesus most certainly was. A mamzer would be excluded from fully participating in the Jewish rituals and refused entry into the synagogue. A mamzer wouldn't be allowed to marry within the established bloodlines of Israel. A mamzer would be an outcast, a reject. A mamzer could easily be drawn into other religious groups that were egalitarian as Jesus did with John the Baptist. A mamzer might even start his own reformation that would seek to break down the barriers enforced by purity laws that had people bound to rules and regulations like the Pharisees and the scribes.

Think of it! Over and over again, Jesus can be seen reaching out to the outcast, welcoming those who were never welcomed, eating with sinners, advocating that no one is excluded from the love of God. This is not the teachings of someone who led a privileged and protected life but rather the teachings of an outsider, one who has been rejected by his religion, a bastard, a mamzer.

DECEMBER 6

"Can anything good come out of Nazareth?" What's that all about if not the reinforcement of Jesus as an outsider? Nathaniel, a good Jewish lad, can hardly fathom how a mamzer of all people, from Nazareth of all places, could be heralded as a great rabbi, the messiah even! This just can't be true!

But it is and that is at the heart of true Christianity. Jesus, the incarnation of God, comes to us not as a religious insider. Not with a clerical collar or a fancy robe. Not with thousands of well-dressed and overly-fed followers. Jesus comes humbled by his circumstance, beaten down by the system, alienated by the people of power. Jesus comes as a mamzer. Jesus comes and proclaims a new understanding, a new reality, a new world and he calls it the kingdom of God. It is a kingdom that is not limited to insiders. It is not just for right believers or clean livers.

It is for everyone. Rich and poor. Jew or Greek. Black or white. Faithful or faithless. Everyone.

DECEMBER 7

I worship for much the same reasons that I do the dishes at home. It renews my relationship with the ones I love and who love me. Reaching out for my lover's hand or for the vacuum cleaner are both expressions of how much I cherish our affair. There are times when I am called to work and other times to simply revel but often it is these little rituals that serve to not only express our love but to build it stronger.

DECEMBER 8

After graduating from seminary and despite my good grades and nice suit, I had an extraordinarily difficult time getting a job. On one particularly depressing evening, I was driving back from a little church in the San Francisco Bay area wondering what it was that had these seemingly Christian people turning their thumbs down on me like Nero in the Coliseum. I figured the moment came when one rather intimidating older gentleman leaned over across the table, pointed his finger a few inches from my nose and growled, "I've heard all about the classes you took and the family you have. Now I just want to know one thing. Do you or do you not believe in the bodily resurrection of Jesus?" In good Lutheran style, I spoke of art and how I believed that the gospel writers were artists who painted with words their deep and utter convictions. Despite the profundity of my own words and the creativity of my reply, the interview came quickly to a conclusion and I was left wondering what I was doing wrong…again.

On the drive back to my home and to a wife who would once again hear that there was another Lutheran congregation not too interested in having her husband as a pastor, I realized where I was going wrong. It harkened back to my enchantment with the world of art. I love the Impressionists and most of Christianity, it seems, would rather spend their time with the Realists. They want facts and figures, names and numbers while I and a few others are happily content with ethereal impressions, suggestive strokes of a broad brush rather than the intricate details of the technician. There is a sense that those of us drawn to impressionism over realism have been swimming up a spiritual stream, or maybe it's more of a religious river. Despite the tide, we believe that Christianity is not based on facts but on faith, not on doctrinal tests but on deep trust.

December 9

How we behave toward others proclaims what we believe about God. All the talk, all the doctrine, all the self-help books on the Christian bookstore shelves mean nothing without action. As much as I love worship, as much as I cherish the liturgy and treasure our songs of faith, if this is all we do on our spiritual journey then our God is a midget who mirrors our own teeny faith.

DECEMBER 10

In recent years, I find myself shying away from images that no longer work. Being washed in the blood of the lamb is one such image. The ancient ritual of standing in a pit while a bleating animal is slaughtered above you and having the blood pour down upon you is hardly a meaningful experience in this day and age. What I have found most helpful in my own spiritual journey is to substitute the word love whenever I came across the word blood in a hymn. It almost always works. See if you don't agree that such a change is far more indicative of your faith, far more a part of the language that you can understand.

DECEMBER 11

Throughout the New Testament whenever Mary Magdalene is mentioned she seems to have a prominent position. Time and again, it is Mary Magdalene who receives prominence in the listing of women. Time and again, Mary Magdalene appears to have a venerated position at least among the women in the story but maybe even among the men as well.

Who is the first to recognize the resurrection of Jesus? Who is the first to have the privilege of seeing the risen Christ? Is it Peter? Is it the mysterious beloved disciple? Is it Andrew or James or John or even the Virgin Mary? No, it is Mary Magdalene, Mary the Great! It is Mary Magdalene who is the very first witness to the resurrection, the very first person to proclaim that Jesus is raised from the dead.

Hypothesis: Mary Magdalene, indeed many other women as well, had a more influential role in the beginnings of the Jesus Movement than we have been led to believe.

DECEMBER 12

So the truth is we change. Usually not all at once, not in one great dramatic swoop, but slowly, with subtle little shifts and faintly nuanced turns. Recently someone said to me in a somewhat pejorative manner, "You've changed." I wondered what they meant by that. I wondered if they were suggesting that it was possible not to change. I wondered if they were being critical of where my spiritual journey has taken me. I wondered about a lot of things but this much I knew for sure. They were right. I have changed, thank God.

DECEMBER 13

The message of Christ is a message of hope. It is imbued with the promise that this living spirit of love never abandons us even in the face of great hatred and horrors. It is the conviction that violence is never the ultimate answer. It is the witness of Jesus who was willing to die rather than strike back in anger. How in the name of Christ can Christians claim the dark and sinister theology of separation and damnation as being from God?

DECEMBER 14

I have had the great pleasure of officiating at a wedding between a Lutheran and a member of the Bahai faith. Now I've done Christian/Buddhist weddings and Christian/Jewish ones. I've married atheists and agnostics, pagans and Presbyterians but never have I had the privilege of even meeting, let alone marrying, a Bahai.

Let me tell you a little about this little known faith. It started in Persia, now known as Iran. Much as Christianity emerged out of Judaism, Bahai grew out of Islam. Curiously some of the basic tenets are very similar to the true heart of Christianity. Its guiding principle is the unification of all people, a recognition that we are all children of God and called to live in harmony with one another. Tribalism is seen as the great threat to this vision of peace. The parallels to the teachings of Jesus are striking especially as we ponder his emphasis on welcoming the outsider. What are most fascinating to me are the houses of worship for Bahais. They are always nine-sided structures that symbolize the diversity of humanity and its oneness. I've read where the aisles that lead to the center of their sanctuaries represent the different religious traditions in our world that all lead to God. Such a theology, as little as I know of it, seems to resonate with much of what Jesus tried to teach his disciples. "Whoever is not against us is for us."

Perhaps this beautiful religion can serve as a guide for Christians as we seek to return to the essential message of Jesus.

DECEMBER 15

One of my mentors, Thich Nhat Hahn, is a Buddhist who teaches, I believe, in the spirit of Jesus. Thich says, "When you grow a tree, if it does not grow well, you don't blame the tree. You look for the reasons it is not doing well. You may need fertilizer, or more water, or less sun. You never blame the tree...yet we blame (people for not turning out the way we'd like.) If we know how to take care of others, they will grow well, like a tree. Blaming has no effect at all. Never blame, never try to persuade using reason and arguments. They never lead to any positive effect. That is my experience. No argument, no reasoning, no blame, just understanding. If you understand, and you show that you understand, you can love, and the situation will change."

December 16

Before he died, Pope John Paul II reminded all his priests that those denominations outside of the Roman Catholic Church, like Lutherans, Presbyterians, Methodists and such, were not to be addressed as "sister churches" since such a description might imply some kind of legitimacy on those denominations.

If the unity of the church depends on the continuing denial of women as equal bearers of the divine image and the continuing oppression and even persecution of our homosexual brothers and sisters then I say I want no part of church unity and, what's more, I dare say you shouldn't either.

DECEMBER 17

One of the most helpful ways of understanding our differences in interpreting the Bible comes from Marcus Borg who writes of a pre-conscious literalism and a post-conscious literalism.

The pre-conscious literalism is the literalism of Jesus' day. The world was flat, the earth was the center of the universe and heaven was just beyond the last star. This was not questioned but was accepted by nearly everyone but the imaginative few. It certainly shouldn't have us criticizing Jesus or anyone else for this world-view. This is how it was. But post-conscious literalism is when we know that the evidence, scientific or otherwise, demands a re-evaluation and yet we continue to hold onto the ancient worldview. Such a position is difficult to defend and yet millions of Christians read the Bible with just such a bias.

DECEMBER 18

We must recognize that being followers of Jesus does not mean that everything always works out the way that we want it. Jesus doesn't tell us that the widow who puts in her last pennies is taken care of and lives happily ever after. For all we know she was still poor and still living on the outside of society. We do know that that is precisely where Jesus chose to live and if that makes us uncomfortable so be it. Let's live with the discomfort. Let's not try and change what Jesus actually did.

DECEMBER 19

Santa Claus is the very antithesis of amazing grace, the very opposite of the gospel message. When do you get a gift…only when you haven't shouted or pouted or cried and been good for goodness sake. But the essence of Christ's teaching was that the gift came unwarranted and unasked. It is never contingent on who you are or what you've done. It is a gift, pure, simple and free. No strings attached. No demands for reciprocity. Grace. Unconditional and amazing.

DECEMBER 20

I suppose "The Magnificat" is one of my favorite passages in the Bible. I have no doubt, however, that Mary did not write and perform it for her cousin Elizabeth or anyone else for that matter.

What this beautiful passage indicates to me is how the early church associated Mary with the poor and oppressed of the world. "The Magnificat" was a hymn of the early church that proclaimed God's overriding bias for the poor. Here was a poor woman living in an occupied country, pregnant and yet to be married. She knows what it is like to be on the outside. She knows what it is like to be among the rejected. What a powerful symbol of the unconditional love of God!

Isn't it odd then that most of us Christians have for two thousand years or so confused worldly success with being blessed by God? If Mary is to be believed, nothing could be further from the truth. There can be no greater honor than to carry Christ within us and the one who symbolizes that for all of us is humble, poor, dispossessed Mary.

We should all be pondering that in our hearts.

DECEMBER 21

There is no mention of the Virgin Mary anywhere in the Bible outside of the two very strange and very different stories in the beginnings of Matthew and Luke. Mary is mentioned elsewhere in the Bible, to be sure, but her description as "Virgin" is never alluded to again. St. Paul, the earliest of writers in the Christian scriptures, says not a word about it. And Mark, the first gospel writer, says nothing either. John, the last of the gospels makes no mention of it. Only Matthew and Luke and neither of them mention it again.

Could it be that the birth of Jesus was a little less dramatic than the fanciful tales we sing and tell at Christmas?

Could it be that the God who we claim works through the ordinary and simple ways of life, did just that? The problem, of course, is that this makes God terribly vulnerable, even powerless. We want a God who can zap the bad guys and make us successful, make us winners. Instead, we get a poor itinerant wanderer who ends up dying like a common criminal. Is it any wonder we want fanciful tales of his birth? It helps us forget that his entire ministry was spent with very ordinary people doing very ordinary things. The miracle of Christ is that in the very ordinariness of it all, God is revealed, the kingdom comes. In the simple actions of love, forgiveness and peacemaking, we enter into the kingdom of heaven. It doesn't take guiding stars, singing shepherds or perpetual virgins to make this true. It is true and it is known as we follow Jesus into the ordinariness of our lives.

DECEMBER 22

Do you find it as curious as I do that we have little trouble, it seems, believing in voices coming out of the sky but enormous difficulty accepting the possibility that God can be heard in every act of kindness and grace? I wonder how many millions of gentle souls have been turned away from the church because we so often deny what Jesus' life and death proclaimed…God comes in vulnerability, openness and love. Surely this is far more important in the story of Mary than her unusual biological condition.

DECEMBER 23

"Oh come, oh, come, Emmanuel, and ransom captive Israel."

What exactly are we asking for there? Sounds like someone needs to pay a ransom for Israel. And you know who that someone is, don't you?

Such sentiment is based on the belief that the primary purpose of Jesus' life was to be killed as a kind of atoning sacrifice to appease a very disappointed God. Much of traditional Christianity still clings to this rather bizarre thinking. Our sin separates us from God and the only way to bridge that separation is for Jesus to die. You figure it out because, quite frankly, I can't. Oh, I've studied the Bible pretty carefully and I've read more theological treatises than most folk but I simply can't accept a worldview that may have made sense two thousand years ago but certainly doesn't today.

Is this really why we sing this song? So Jesus can come and pay a ransom to God? I'd rather sing of the Jesus who came not to die some prearranged death but to show us how to live.

DECEMBER 24

There's a wonderful old story not in the Bible but it could be.

A Yankee is driving through the deep south and he pulls in to a little roadside cafe for some breakfast. The waitress takes his order of flapjacks, fried eggs and bacon. But when the meal arrives, besides his fried eggs, flap-jacks and bacon there is this white, lumpy concoction in the corner of his plate. He called the waitress over and asked her,

"What in the world is that stuff?"

"Why sir, them's grits."

"But I didn't order them.", he told her.

With a big smile, the waitress reassured him, "Sir, you don't order grits. They just come!"

That's the way it is with God's grace. Abundant. Extravagant, Prodigal. It just comes.

DECEMBER 25

Marcus Borg once said, "Show me your image of God and I will show you your theology." People who think God is angry at the world will more than likely be angry at the world as well. People who think that God is a warrior king will more than likely be ready willing and able to wage war in the name of that God. People who think God is exactly like what they think God is exactly like are more than likely not going to be open to any other images of God that matter to others.

DECEMBER 26

A friend and I were talking recently. It had been a while since we had seen each other so we were catching up on this and that and then he said to me something that was clearly on his mind and causing him no little consternation. He said, "You know Rich, I don't think I have any faith any more." As you can imagine, that put a little damper on the conversation, at least one level of the conversation. I asked him what he meant by faith, what kind of faith didn't he have any more. "You know", he said. "God up there sending Jesus down here to die for our sins." It was a pretty classic understanding of Christian belief but, I told him, it is not the only understanding of Christianity. And then, whether he liked it or not, I launched into a rather lengthy explanation of how Christianity slowly grew out of a myriad of different understandings of the life and death and resurrection of Jesus. The one he described became, of course, the dominant belief but, I thought he needed to know; it is not the only belief.

DECEMBER 27

I met Joseph Sittler in one of the last years of his life. He was a brilliant theologian who was also a Lutheran and for me at that time that was almost an oxymoron. Dr. Sittler never published a great theological tome, only a few small collections of some of his sermons and reflections from his well-used notebook. In his final years, Sittler had gone almost completely blind. He needed an assistant to help him walk across campus, open his mail, read his books. The fact that the assistants were almost invariably very attractive young co-eds sometimes had me questioning just how blind he really was. In any case, I was taking a seminar from him at the Lutheran Seminary in Chicago and we got to talking about hymns and what was then the introduction of the new Lutheran Book of Worship. Dr. Sittler listened to the arguments among the various members of the class as to what hymns were appropriate and which were not and then he interrupted the discussion with what I thought was a very insightful comment. He said since he was blind as a bat he couldn't see the words anyway and so all the arguing meant little to him. In fact, he said, "I just sing the alphabet along with the tune and I dare say I get as much out of the song as any of you and probably more so." And then he demonstrated…"A B C D E F G H I J K L M N…". He made a point, a very good and appropriate point.

DECEMBER 28

Grace. It is a wonderful word that is both noun and verb, adjective and adverb. But more than anything else it is a reminder that we are called, all of us who boldly bear the name of Christian, to live in a spirit of thanksgiving, grateful to a God who is so gracious to us. Grace. It is a wonderful word. It is an even more wonderful way of living.

DECEMBER 29

On the day Merton died, he was speaking before a gathering of monks from all different traditions. He said this to them, "My brothers and sisters, we are already one. We only imagine we are different. What we have to become is what we are." You see, this is the heart of the spiritual journey for Merton. It is to become what we are. I'll never forget preparing to receive the Holy Eucharist out in Grace Cathedral in San Francisco and hearing the celebrant, Alan Jones, declare as he broke the host, "See who you are. Become what you see." That is salvation for Merton and, I humbly say, for me. To become what we are and what we are is the image of God.

Merton again: "There is only one problem on which all my existence, my peace and my happiness depend: to discover myself in discovering God, if I find Him I will find myself and if I find my true self I will find Him."

DECEMBER 30

For way too long we in the church have been uncomfortable with imagination and Christianity. Over the past two millennia there have been systematic and concerted efforts on the part of some folk to stamp out imagination entirely from the church. If all the questions are already answered, if all the mystery is already solved, there's no need for imagination. That is why some Christians are so bent on blocking out imagination. It confuses our nice neat little answers. It takes us places it may be dangerous to go. 500 years ago Martin Luther imagined a God whose love was unconditional, whose grace was undiminished and what happened? He got chucked out of the church. Imagination is a wonderful but dangerous thing. It was the driving force behind the Reformation and it must continue to drive the church of today. A church without imagination worships a dead God. A church without imagination finds itself turned inward, afraid of new ideas, new possibilities, new ways of doing things, new ways of imaging God.

DECEMBER 31

What a tragedy that so many of us in the church have been trained to think that doubt is bad. What sadness has been perpetrated, how many searching folk have been driven away by the kind of sanctimonious smugness that pervades too much of Christianity. Don't you find it odd that we in the church get uncomfortable when people confess their doubts, even doubts about some very fundamental matters of faith, and yet we all realize that America was discovered by Christopher Columbus because he doubted when everyone else knew the world was really flat. America itself came into being because men like Washington and Jefferson doubted the universally accepted divine right of kings. Millions of African-American men and women were profoundly helped on their road to equality because Rosa Parks doubted the conventional wisdom that black folk had to sit in the back of the bus. C'mon! Doubt is what makes the world turn! Why are so many in the church afraid of it?

978-0-595-37298-0
0-595-37298-8